Praise for other titles by Jess Phillips

Everything You Really Need to Kno
Life as an MP

'Chatty and anecdotal'
The Times Magazine

'A robustly autobiographical, entertaining attempt to demystify life in Westminster'
Observer

'Honest, funny and very revealing. Her conclusion in particular, "Why we need politics", is essential'
Adam Kay

'Funny and really readable'
Jeremy Vine (BBC Radio Two)

Truth to Power: How to Call Time on Bullsh*t, Speak Up & Make a Difference

'Someone like Jess Phillips in politics does a powerful thing. It makes millions of women like her think, "If she can do politics, maybe I could do politics too."'
Caitlin Moran

'There's nobody else at Westminster quite like Jess Phillips. She is fearless and funny, riotous and rebellious, maverick and mischievous.'
The Times

'Will ruffle some feathers.'
Stylist

Everywoman: One Woman's Truth About Speaking the Truth

'Jess Phillips writes like she talks: brilliantly. Her humour and passion shine through every page. Loved it.'
Robert Webb

'Joyfully candid and very funny.'
Guardian

'Jess Phillips knows the truth . . . and here she shows how scary and sad as well as joyful and liberating the answers can be.'
Damian Barr

'Lord knows we need more MPs like Jess Phillips. As fresh as mountain air amid the Westminster tumbleweed.'
Metro

'A narrative that is by turns witty and furious.'
Gabby Hinsliff, *Guardian* Best Political Books of the Year

'Arresting.'
Observer

LET'S BE HONEST

LET'S BE HONEST

JESS PHILLIPS

GALLERY BOOKS UK

First published in Great Britain by Gallery Books,
an imprint of Simon & Schuster UK Ltd, 2024

3 5 7 9 10 8 6 4 2

Simon & Schuster UK Ltd
1st Floor
222 Gray's Inn Road
London WC1X 8HB

Simon & Schuster: Celebrating 100 Years of Publishing in 2024

www.simonandschuster.co.uk
www.simonandschuster.com.au
www.simonandschuster.co.in

Simon & Schuster Australia, Sydney
Simon & Schuster India, New Delhi

A CIP catalogue record for this book
is available from the British Library

Hardback ISBN: 978-1-3985-0093-8
eBook ISBN: 978-1-3985-0094-5

Typeset in Bembo by M Rules
Printed and Bound in the UK using 100% Renewable Electricity
at CPI Group (UK) Ltd

For Holly Lynch,
who is everything that is right about politics

Contents

Introduction

'Politicians lie' is not an original thought, it's not even a modern refrain; it has been the commonly agreed view for . . . well, for ever. When I was a kid, I remember people chanting 'pigs might fly and politicians lie'. Spin was what we started to call this lying in the modern era of 24-hour news and social media. Spin is different to lying – it is polishing a turd to make it look like a chocolate bar. It is not necessarily a *lie*; it can be a diversionary tactic by focusing on the tiniest bit of positive, or an attempt to distract from the facts by talking about something else entirely, or getting the bad news out on a day when no one is watching, like releasing terrible data on prison deaths on the day of the World Cup final. But it's all lying to me and should be warded against.

However, the art of political spin and the occasional mega porky of previous eras is now on amphetamines wearing rocket boosters and travelling at warp speed. Lying has become so commonplace in our politics that I can hardly believe a single thing that I am told. Lying became the standard and approved way to survive in politics, where the act of governing all but gave way to the art of political war. Winning elections is deeply important. I am not one of those idealists who believe in purity above practicality, and that the need to offer people enough stuff to get them to vote for you is a sin. You can deliver nothing from opposition; it is not a virtue. But the priority of fighting electoral battles and wedge-issue skirmishes over actually doing the job of making the world a better place has enabled a culture where lying thrives and progress falters.

But I am a democrat. I want to make it clear that I am such a zealot about the act and art of democracy that I have thought about it every single day of my life. Much of my childhood was dedicated to elections. Every room in the house had 'Vote Labour' posters piled up in the corners, and we had an old-fashioned crank-operated duplicator in our garage, where local councillors would come and churn out inky leaflets with messages about Labour Party campaigns for local, national and international elections, or about the miners or Mrs Thatcher snatching our milk. I went to a women's liberation playgroup, for God's sake, a political childcare movement set up by local Labour women so that other women could work and campaign and stand for office. My grandfather, who was an artist, used to make me stand in poses for hours so he could get the political cartoons he was drawing for the socialist campaign group just right. I was raised on a picket line.

I love democracy deeply. To live in a country where the people truly have the power to change individual laws (please see any of my other books for how this does happen and you are being conned by powerful bad-faith actors if you don't think it does), to rid themselves of bad leaders, and to strike a blow against the establishment with the simple act of voting is so utterly delicious to me.

Don't believe me? Look at how efficiently our democracy saw off the undemocratically elected Liz Truss in short order. No sooner was she dusting off her coat of mourning having laid the Queen* to rest, than she was packing up her bags and shipping out. History will be written about that era in politics in which the role of the people was all but ignored. We will hear tales of secret plotting, hushed tones in dark corners, and the solemn, serious words of the chair of the 1922 Committee† about how Liz Truss did not have the confidence of the Conservative and Unionist Parliamentary Party. Column inch after column inch will record how a sober man called Jeremy Hunt had to step in and take charge of an out-of-control woman who was slashing taxes and ripping up our great nation's rule book of financial policy.

---

* Insert your own joke about how we live in a democracy with a monarch. I am not a monarchist; I was raised by socialists with Irish heritage, so you can imagine the views I inherited. However, I can say with some confidence that had I had to vote for a head of state I probably would have voted for the Queen. She was epic, and if you can find me a British citizen who would have not interfered with our democracy with such grace then I'll vote for them too.

† The 1922 Committee is the name for all Conservative Party backbenchers. Wikipedia informs me that it was formed in 1923, which seems odd. The Labour Party has a similar body called the Parliamentary Labour Party (PLP), which is run by the backbench committee of the PLP. Trust the Tories to have a name that sounds olde-worlde and as if only men in oak-panelled rooms would be invited.

When the men in grey suits aren't given the credit for saving our country the markets will wear the crown. Truss spooked the financial markets and sent the pound tumbling and interest rates soaring. She increased my mortgage payments by £700 per month – a fact I like to remind her of with an accumulating total each time I see her walking as if butter wouldn't melt through the vaulted halls of Westminster.* 'Liz, you owe me £13,000, I'll take a cheque.' It was the markets that did her in, no economic event so nuclear could be ignored, and so the faceless market men did their work and made sure she was gone. They needed confidence, you see; an unconfident market cannot stand.

These things are all true, no doubt about it. The men in grey suits did visit Liz Truss with her death warrant, the markets did go absolutely apeshit, but had she had the support of the people in our country, had she been popular with the public, had they thought that in fact millionaires *did* deserve a tax cut bigger than the wage of a nurse, or that bankers had frankly had it too tough for too long on their limited bonuses,† then Liz Truss would have remained the prime minister.

---

* Liz Truss must be glad she gets a security detail for life having been PM because I never see anyone else walking with her in Westminster. Thank God she has a secret agent in case she can't get the zip of an awkward dress done up.

† I spoke to loads of bankers at the time – you see, we do that as politicians because they are not all bogeymen and are quite important to our economy – and every single one was horrified by Liz Truss's suggestions concerning bankers' bonuses. They, the super-rich, thought it was stupid and tin-eared.

The people accurately thought she was a dangerous lunatic. To be fair to the people, they thought that before the Tories elected her as their leader, and they thought it all the way through the Tory leadership contest, but in a flaw in our democracy they didn't get a say. Instead, we the public just got to watch on in horror, only alleviated slightly by sharing videos of her views on cheese and pork markets. To this day my son, who was fourteen at the time, can repeat Liz Truss's entire conference speech about the 'disgraceful' level of cheese imports, thanks to amusing video mashups on TikTok.

In my constituency of Birmingham Yardley there was, at the time of Truss's Conservative leadership, one member of the Conservative Party. She is a lovely woman in fairness to her, does good for the community and is well liked as best I can tell. She is always kind to me. We did have another one for a spell, but he left over Brexit. I am working on the assumption that it's now just this solitary woman.* This one woman was the only person in my constituency who got to pick the nation's prime minister on behalf of everyone in Birmingham Yardley. I joked at the time that I might publish her email address for the other 120,000 people in the area to have their say, or at least the 90,000 electors. Obviously, this would be a gross breach of data protection and while I, as the elected representative, do have to tolerate this scrutiny it seemed a little unfair on her. But the

---

* I could be wrong, there could be loads, they don't invite me to their shindigs. However, the one who left over Brexit told me he only knew of him and her.

point stands; it was not the people who made this gross mistake over Liz Truss (apart from those in South West Norfolk – someone should have a very stern word with them). It was a tiny group of Conservative Party members.

The country's visceral reaction of at best ridicule and at worst fear meant that Liz Truss had to go. She could not command the confidence of the public. For me personally it would have been better if she'd stayed; she was gold to a Labour politician and the day she was elected I raised a glass to Conservative stupidity. That jubilation lasted until I got the massive mortgage bill and people in my constituency who had not struggled previously started telling me that they were spending their savings just to live and that their dreams of home ownership were now in the dustbin with the prime minister's dignity. Short-term pleasure and revelry always bite back, and the hangover was so bad on this one that I should never have raised a wry smile.

The people and their lives did for Liz Truss. The markets and the grey suits were merely their postmen. Democracy, you see, it keeps things in check. As I said, I am a huge fan, I've signed up to the fanzine, I pay my subs, I queue in the cold for democracy . . . hell, I'll stay up all night in its service.

However, it is not immune to being subverted by lying politicians. I cannot count the ways; however, in the pursuit of better, I will try.

The period of Tory rule starting in 2010 was the most destructive Conservative government I have lived under, and I was born under Thatcher. It may well be that this shower of shit made literally zero positive progress for our country other than gay marriage – which, to be fair, was carried through on Labour votes because at the time too many of their own majority were busy hand-wringing about how it might mean we end up with a gay monarch and the succession of the crown would be in jeopardy, like some sort of *Game of Thrones* battle. Bring on the dragons, I say. Other than that, they just destroyed stuff like a bunch of crazed toddlers in a sweet shop with a baseball bat. So many years wasted.

I was elected in an era of growing populism and mis-information, and it is my view that in the pursuit of popularity rather than satisfaction, politics, and democracy itself, is broken. In a wham-bam-thank-you-ma'am media environment of 24-hour news and social media dominance we are retweeting away the long-term changes and polit-ical stability we all claim to want to see.

Unless we sort out the issue of how people interact with democracy globally, we are heading for danger. In 2023 the Open Society Foundations undertook an international survey of thirty countries. They found that while 86 per cent of respondents would prefer to live in a democratic state, only 57 per cent of respondents aged eighteen to thirty-five felt democracy was preferable to any other form of government. They also found that more than a third (35 per cent) of young people felt a 'strong leader' who did not hold elections or consult parliament was 'a good way to run a country'.

In a *Guardian* article written about the findings of the

survey it was reported that Mark Malloch-Brown, OSF's president and a former UN deputy secretary-general, said: 'People around the world still want to believe in democracy, but generation by generation that faith is fading as doubts grow about its ability to deliver concrete changes to their lives.' This is a problem we are storing up for the future. Young people, who, it is no coincidence, live much more of their lives online, are falling out of love with the very idea of democracy. In 2022 the Institute for Public Policy Research (IPPR) think tank, in partnership with the *Observer* newspaper, undertook a similar survey into attitudes towards democracy. This too showed a problem of future-proofing, with young UK adults (18–24) being least likely to think that democracy served them well (just 19 per cent saying it operated well, against 55 per cent who said it operated badly).

If I, a democratic zealot, can see how broken our democratic system is, it is no longer enough just to sit back and rest on the laurels of the Winston Churchill quote: 'Democracy is the worst form of government except for all those other forms that have been tried from time to time.'

Do I think we should have longer term lengths? Nope, if anything they seem too long. Am I proposing merely a governance structure free from electoral constraint? Absolutely not, that is a dictatorship, and I don't care how many people turn up quickly and efficiently to fix a pothole in China,* I prefer freedom.

---

* I kid you not. Once while on a delegation to Beijing, back before that was a thing that would have been considered unthinkable, I watched seven men changing the lightbulb of a streetlamp that wasn't working.

The only way forward is to end the era of political lying once and for all. Politicians need to clean up their act. And the public and the press must stop joining in with the charade that places populist policies, dividing lines and charismatic political leadership above boring old service delivery. Our cravings must move from the desire for a delicious instant hit to something that will actually sustain us.

I

Smoke and Mirrors

As I am writing this, in January 2024, I'm in my bed in the spare room of my house. I have been banished from my normal sleeping quarters because I have a cough so bad it could wake the dead. My husband has fared poorly trying to sleep next to me as he is both alive and quite a light sleeper. Sticky pools of Night Nurse are congealing on the bedside table and an assorted number of inhalers and packets of steroids and antibiotics peep out among the debris of screwed-up bog roll and cold cups of tea. I am sick, so sick, in fact, that I was forced to attend Queen Elizabeth Hospital A&E department in Birmingham. After my lips went blue and I couldn't catch my breath, and having been ill for six weeks, I decided that breathing was a luxury I should strive for. So, at 10 p.m. on the day after Boxing Day, I took myself off to the hospital.

You may remember this hospital; it featured in a political fracas involving Tony Blair. You see, it was the last Labour government that built this brand-spanking-new hospital.

From where I live you can see its enormity as a site on the landscape. It is huge. Tony Blair came to the hospital for a manifesto launch in 2001, obviously wanting to show what governance looks like – a massive hospital that resembles a spaceship. Sharon Storer, whose partner was a cancer patient at the hospital, attacked the then PM about there not being enough nurses and beds. She said her partner's treatment in the A&E unit had been 'absolutely disgusting'. Ah, the people – not even happy when you build a massive new hospital and waiting times are just four hours long. I will return to Sharon Storer and her noble activism, but back to my time in this hospital.

I arrived at the door of A&E and through the window I could see that the waiting area was standing room only. In the dark and cold December evening I didn't even make it across the threshold as in the lobby (the small area between two sets of sliding doors) sat a nurse at a 'vitals testing' station. This nurse was going to decide my fate by how well I did on an oxygen level test and heart-rate readout. Would I be allowed to enter? Was I really ill enough? I was hooked up to the machine while Storm Gerrit* blew a gale into the lobby, which was completely exposed to the elements by one set of doors being permanently open. Luckily, I failed or in fact passed the test because my resting heart rate was 129 beats per minute and my blood oxygen level

---

* Why did we start naming all the storms? Seriously, they got so wildly above their station when we started naming every gust of wind. Ignore the scientists telling you it is climate change causing all this crazy weather – I think the naming is to blame.

was between 94 and 95 per cent depending on whether my shellac nail polish was affecting the machine. I was low on oxygen (no shit, my lips had turned blue) and my heart was having a mare. I was cleared for entry, but not to the waiting room, which was full. I was sent back outside (remember the storm and my poorly heart) to walk to another waiting area two doors down and about a hundred metres away. I went to where ambulance patients were being admitted. Presumably, there was more space there because there were no sodding ambulances anymore.

In the new, also full, waiting room, I sat on a hard plastic chair next to a woman who had waited for an ambulance for eight hours as she was in searing pain in her stomach following a recent operation on her womb. The ambulance never came so she was instructed to try to make her own way there. I was grateful to this woman, who was in full pyjamas, slippers and dressing gown, as I had been a little worried about the fact that I was wearing pyjama bottoms because, as an elected representative of many of the people in this waiting room, it is bad form to wear nightclothes in public. No one batted an eyelid. These people had bigger fish to fry than the sartorial stylings of a wheezing MP.

People did look at me in surprise, as if being a Member of Parliament means I do not get ill, or that when I do, I am not entitled to some secret amazing hospital where all my needs are immediately catered for. People genuinely think that MPs don't rely on the same services as everyone else. Some don't, obviously. Rishi Sunak – whose family is worth billions of pounds – would probably have been able to access the meds he needed in the first six weeks of his chronic breathing illness. Also, the super-rich just are not as chronically ill, because they have houses in the countryside and leisure facilities and professionals to call on at a moment's notice. But most MPs use the National Health Service just like everyone else. Rishi Sunak only uses the NHS because he was shamed into it by Laura Kuenssberg from the BBC asking him if he did. He pretended that it was a private matter, which it was, very much a private affair for him. In sheer cynical embarrassment he duly registered with an NHS GP in a bid to look normal in between private-jet flights and planning disputes over his swimming pools.

I do not use private healthcare so, following a once-over from a nurse in A&E, I was moved to another area called 'sub-wait'. Sub-wait is obviously the least good of the now three waiting areas; it hasn't made the major leagues, it is subpar. In here there were twice as many people as in both previous waiting areas. I spotted some of those who had made it through the original lobby and some people who had been brought in by paramedics; all of us were now relegated to sub-wait. Here I sat next to a young man who looked in pain and told me he had been in sub-wait for six hours. I kid you not, when he told me this I said, 'Oh, not too bad.'

Three months prior to this trip to the hospital I had spent seventeen hours in the waiting room with my octogenarian father who was so racked with an infection he had become delirious and kept collapsing. He had tried and failed over the previous week to get a GP appointment, until he ended up on the verge of developing sepsis, which for an elderly man with blood cancer is, like this waiting room, suboptimal. So, six hours seemed pretty good to me.

After a stint in sub-wait I was seen by a doctor and was to be moved out of the waiting-room roulette to an area where I'd receive some actual treatment. Hooray!* In the days that Tony Blair would have been visiting this hospital in 2001 these treatment rooms were individual cubicles. I know because I visited at the time with an acute stomach issue that once again made my dodgy heart race too fast. I was put in a cubicle to be given fluids and meds, and my mate Alex sat alongside me. Same thing when my husband broke his leg in 2004: bit of a wait then moved off into the cubicle area for a consultation before being sent for an X-ray. But this was 2023, not 2004, so I was put in the cubicle to be hooked up to a nebuliser in order to clear my chest, which by now sounded like I was a walking bagpipe with every step that I took. I will say something for this room: the chairs all around the outside of the cubicle, of which there were nine, were cushioned which felt like a spot of luxury.

---

* I have to be honest here. I only waited in both waiting rooms for three hours in total. This is because I was given special treatment. There is no doubt about it, it was even said to me. I tried to rebuff the offer but was told that it wasn't fair when I was so ill to leave me in the waiting room where people were starting to appeal to me with their issues. I was becoming a focus of attention, as I had when my father was ill. However, on that occasion I was absolutely fine and was happy to sit and help others in the waiting room I shared with them for seventeen hours. On this occasion I could not be so helpful.

I was in this cubicle area with, among others, a young pregnant woman who was suffering in her second pregnancy, as she had in her first, with hyperemesis gravidarum. This basically means you cannot keep down any food or fluids; it is very dangerous if untreated and she did not look very pregnant to me, she was a bag of bones. I sat in the chair next to her. I could not see her face as she was doubled over, trying to sleep, arm hooked up to a drip of medicine and fluids. When her drip stopped, she did try to flag a passing nurse, who explained that there were three of them on shift for sixty patients. The gaunt pregnant woman tried to sip some water she had brought with her and then promptly started to vomit. I imagine I had stopped her sleeping, since I was next to her hooked up to a nebuliser that was whirring louder than my vacuum cleaner does and spewing out vapour like I was in some Victorian laudanum den. (Chance would have been a fine thing. One woman was wailing in the corridors that after eight hours she had not been offered so much as a paracetamol; she'd have given her right arm for a blast of laudanum.)

Now, it would be one thing if only me and this woman were in this cubicle meant for one, breaking every single cardinal rule about the privacy you might be afforded in a medical setting, but we were just two of six other patients in said cubicle, all hooked up to various machines, with their beeps and whirrs. I want to reiterate that this was not a ward, this was a cubicle *for one*. Once upon a time this would have had a bed, a chair for a friend, partner or concerned child, and some equipment for the clinical staff.

Why a woman who has a diagnosed condition, who knew exactly the meds she needed, could not have been managed by community maternity services rather than clogging up A&E in the middle of the night away from her 14-month-old baby, in a hospital a stone's throw from the actual maternity hospital, is literally the riddle of the goddamn sphinx. But he we all are.

In order to offer some privacy to her and my other fellow patients and their machines, I did what anyone does to try to become invisible – I stared at my mobile phone. It was that time of night when the headlines for the next day are revealed and, on this occasion, I was treated to the second go on the merry-go-round of Jeremy Hunt's big idea to get rid of inheritance tax.

In this little cubicle my pregnant friend and I were younger than all of our chairfellows by at least thirty years. Four elderly women in varying slumped states joined us. Only one of them was accompanied to the hospital, by her adult daughter. The accompanied woman was hooked up to an oxygen mask that her daughter kept helping her with while trying to remain jolly through the worry. They had been there since 2 p.m. It was now midnight. I didn't – because it would have been crass in the worrying circumstances – but I wanted to ask her if, when she looked at her mother trying to sleep and struggling for breath, what she saw was dollar signs. Like a cartoon character sees their prey always as a steaming leg of ham. Was a sick elderly relative now just a route to financial security?

I am, of course, making massive assumptions about how

wealthy this woman was. She had a very nice jumper on and the neat bob of a woman who took care of herself. I had little else to go on. If I had to be so base as to guess, this woman was the only other person in our crowded cubicle for one with any real assets to trouble the inheritance tax collectors. But over a million quid? Nope, not a chance. I mean, it was a nice jumper but not that nice. What do I know, she could have been a property magnate with loads of assets worth far and above the price of the average house in the city she lives in, which then stood at £269,039. If she was the average Birmingham homeowner, she would fall well below the threshold to pay any inheritance tax at all. Even if she wanted to leave her house to a complete stranger no tax would be due as the threshold is £325,000, and that is before you get another £175,000 tax relief if you leave it to your kids. And if your partner died before you, you store up their tax relief, which is also £325,000 plus £175,000, so a million quid in most families.

Funnily enough, I know this because my almost communist father commented, while he was on his epic seventeen-hour wait just months before, that at least if he died that day the state would get some cash to try to sort out the mess he saw before him. While he bought his home for £33,000 in the 1980s, it is now worth over half a million quid as the area he bought in gentrified around him (as gentrified as Birmingham gets, that is). I had to disappoint him in his fragile condition and tell him that in fact the state wouldn't get a penny, because while he, a man born in a council house, had done pretty well for himself, he was only top 10 per cent wealthy from un-earned income compared to his countrymen and you have to be strictly top 4 per cent to qualify to pay any inher-itance tax. Frankly, the fact he had never double-glazed his windows, or decided to move with the times where people have showers not just baths (for him the idea of an ensuite was so bourgeois as to be vulgar), had kept his heirs and successors free from the burden of the taxman.

So disgusted was my father by this turn of events that meant that none of his assets would be going back to the solid earth of the state that he treated the whole waiting room to a lecture on the curses of inheritance and un-earned income. It's painting by numbers for him; he's been making that speech since 1963.

Inheritance tax, you see, is only paid by the very wealthy. There are undoubtedly some flaws in the system: cohabit-ing siblings, for example, cannot have the same benefits as married couples. It is not perfect and could do with a bit of a once-over but ultimately hardly anyone pays it. Last time Jeremy Hunt waded out with this stupid idea I looked up the properties then for sale in my constituency and only one was over the initial threshold amount of £325,000 and none was more than the £500,000 that a single person leaving their estate to their children would have to reach.

The juxtaposition of reading this headline while being in this near-warzone-like emergency medical situation (I have genuinely visited more private spacious medical facil-ities in refugee camps in the developing world) maddened me. There I was, sat in a service on its knees because of a failure of governance, planning and resource over the previous decade, six years of which Jeremy Hunt himself had been in charge of the Department of Health, and his big idea was a cut in a tax that 96 per cent of the population would never pay at a cost of billions to the country. The failure was breathtaking, which in my condition then was not ideal.

Where the hell were his big brave bold ideas when he was health secretary about community-based maternity services that would have saved that young woman from having to stoop over and vomit in front of strangers? Where was the decade-long public health reform that would have stopped the heroin addicts desperately stalking the hall of this A&E unit, in and out of the cubicle I sat in? Where the fuck was the social care reform that would have avoided four elderly women, gasping for oxygen, confused, distressed and mostly alone, ending up sitting in a tiny, dirty room with vomiting, breathless, noisy patients?

If I had been crass enough to raise the issue of inheritance tax with the worried daughter propping up her mother's oxygen tank, I'd have asked her if she would rather pay £10,000 in inheritance tax while still receiving a solid quarter of a million pounds she didn't earn, in exchange for a free-at-the-point-of-delivery social care service that would have had her mother's health monitored in her own profit-spiralling home, and have saved her from the indignity she was currently enduring ten hours into her wait. I am almost completely certain that this woman, who looked at the thick end of life and is probably nearing paying off her own mortgage (she too had a nice jumper and a lovely coat), would have been very clear.

I get it, some of you may be reading this and thinking it's all well and good for those who don't have to pay inheritance tax to be against cutting it. Well, sorry to disappoint you because, while I will be dead and therefore my feelings on the matter will be null and void, my kids will likely have to pay it. Not much, you understand, just 40 per cent of anything over the million quid that I imagine my house (which was not bought for anywhere near that amount) will be worth at the time of my passing. Let's say £1.1 million. So, they will have to pay £40,000 in tax while taking home a solid £530,000 **each** that they did naff all to earn, and in fact if anything put some decent effort at teenage parties into reducing the value of my house. All they did was cost me money and all they will get is shedloads of money. Frankly, the £20,000 they each would pay today doesn't seem like enough for the cost they have caused me and the state. They are definitely getting my household quota of nice jumpers. Here I am in the top 4 per cent and my jumpers largely come from H&M or Vinted.

Jeremy Hunt's inheritance tax announcement is a fucking stupid idea, it will not happen. But he had another motive. He announced it at the same time as revealing that the spring budget – usually in April or May – would, in 2024, actually be in March, because he wanted a chance before a possible May election to give out some baubles to voters. We call these 'retail offers'. They are not the big landscape policy ideas like NHS reform, they are things like free childcare and income tax cuts. Hilariously, the Labour Party Twitter[*] account was once hacked before the 2015 election and a retail offer of a free owl for every household was announced. Basically, stuff in your pocket rather than big infrastructure. Cutting inheritance tax is a bauble to those in London and the Home Counties, where people are more asset-rich.

Hunt announced this because he wanted to create a dividing line. Not as the foundations to build anything, not even to win votes, because I suspect not even he is stupid enough to think that he could force a general election win on a voter coalition of people with houses worth more than 2 million quid – you'd be pushed to win just one seat on these numbers even in his Surrey seat.[†] It was merely an act of division. He did it because he wanted the Labour Party to come out and slag it off. He wanted to be able to paint Labour as a party that doesn't believe in strivers; he wanted to try to portray the Labour Party ahead of an election as wanting to steal your children's birthright.

The Labour Party's stance is that while the nation's debt is spiralling, and people wait twelve hours on a floor in a pool of their own excrement for an ambulance that never comes, handing another £30,000 to a rich kid who has already inherited a million quid is not the priority we would

---

[*]   By Twitter I mean X: I refuse to use this terminology partly because it was invented by a manbaby desperate to sound cutting-edge, and also because it is fucking stupid. 'Twitter' literally means to speak – what does X mean other than sounding slightly porny?

[†]   First rule of politics – learn to count!

choose right now. The Tory meme machine can crank out the message: 'DANGER – Labour are going to steal your house!!!'

I reiterate, this was not going to happen, they were not going to abolish inheritance tax; they had no intention of abolishing inheritance tax, they just wanted to let it be known for the sake of electioneering that they think you should keep all the money that you have. Not money that you earned, by the way – the vast majority of wealth people store up in their properties was not earned. They paid their mortgage with their salary, yes, but they also didn't have to sleep on the streets in that time; the money was in exchange for shelter and warmth. I have made nearly £350,000 in the seven years I have lived in my house by doing absolutely nothing, as if the bricks just shit out money. If anything, the reason that my house value has gone up is because of taxpayer-funded infrastructure building in my area. Where I live, we are due a brand-new railway station that will link into the new high-speed rail line to London. My area essentially became a suburb of London while I was living here. The state (and I pay plenty of taxes at a considerably higher proportion of my income than billionaire Rishi Sunak does) helped me make more money. I am not against this; I am just loath to think that my good luck means that, somehow, I earned this wealth. I didn't. I was not big, I was not clever. I was lucky.

I know this is a stark and brutal example of election-eering and, yes, it is worse in the twelve-month run-up to an election, but I cannot express enough that if I had been able to inhale enough breath sat in that crumbling hospital department to scream at the top of my lungs about everything that is wrong with our politics, I would have. Why on earth was running this hospital as part of our treasured National Health Service not the thing that would win votes? This once shiny new hospital, which my own late mother had spent years and years working studiously with others in our local health bureaucracies to ensure was built and would actually serve the local community, felt very personal to me.

You see, my mom cared so much about the health of our city, dedicated her life to trying to make it better, especially when it came to mental health provision, for which a spanking-new facility was also built on this hospital site. She didn't need anyone to vote for her as she sat for hours poring over paperwork and plans; she didn't even get paid for half the work she did volunteering on boards and working groups to get healthcare delivered in our community. I remember her telling me, with tears in her eyes, about the infant mortality rates in parts of the poorest bits of Birmingham. She told me she would not rest until the situation improved. I was so inspired by her drive in this area that while I was pregnant with my first baby, I volunteered to work with pregnant asylum seekers, back then mainly from Rwanda and Sierra Leone, in a scheme to ensure that they were able to access all the care they needed. My mother died in 2011; she passed away at home having recently been discharged into hospice care from that very same hospital she had fought to build. It wasn't perfect, but my God was it in a better state when she left it than when I walked out of it on that cold December night. Her heart wouldn't have just raced at the situation there, it would have broken clean in two.

Reading about the inheritance tax dividing line electioneering while in the hospital made me irate because it's just the kind of ploy that feels so much like a game rather than what politics should be – a job. To me personally it feels more like a vocation, an itch I can never quite scratch sufficiently, something that must be done in the pursuit of better outcomes for the people of our country and around the world. Corny, right? A fair system of governance delivered with, by and for the people. This is the actual inheritance I got from my parents. But I don't even want it to be so romantically celebrated like a Hippocratic oath or a pledge of allegiance. I just want it to be about service delivery and progress, and I don't even want that to be perfect; I just want it to be satisfactory – for it to work.

Electioneering is undoubtedly necessary, I am not pretending that I don't do it too. I do. In the 2015 election, on the subject of my opponent in Birmingham Yardley, I repeated the line, 'He voted for a tax cut for millionaires like him on the very same day he voted for the bedroom tax for people like you' so many times I was saying it in my sleep. Dividing lines matter, but they cannot be all there is. They have to coexist alongside doing the actual job of governing the country.

Sat gasping for breath in that hospital cubicle, with nurses being insulted by desperate patients while Jeremy

Hunt and Rishi Sunak were out electioneering on inheritance tax, made me desperately despondent about the political system I am part of. It brought into sharp focus how ill-served the public are by the democratic system that I love. That arguments between two political ideologies and the need to get out the most damaging meme about your opponent have become so much more important than standing on a platform of boring, straight-up, nothing-to-write-home-about public services.

Of course, it would be impossible for Jeremy Hunt to even try to stand on a platform of good delivery in public services given the Tories' woeful record, the man is not an idiot. But why have we as the people not made this the most basic expectation, a hurdle you have to jump over before you can even contemplate doing the fun stuff and playing the political game of 'your ideology or mine'? When did solid, expected outcomes for the country start to play second fiddle to 'INSERT THREE-WORD SLOGAN HERE', and why did we allow it to happen?

The first problem this comparison between electioneering and just doing a good job of governance throws up for me is one I have to face head-on and just admit to. If the health service had been utterly perfect when I interacted with it that night, I would still never vote Conservative. I am not sure what they would have to do to make someone like me vote for them. If all had been fine and dandy my praise would have gone to the brilliant and caring staff in our health service, which was introduced by my lot, the Labour Party, don't you know.

Tribal politics is a sickness, in my view. A sickness I am very much afflicted by. Luckily, dear reader, I am one of a dying breed of people being killed off by this sickness. Tribal politics is fracturing all over the place and parliamentary seats that had never, since their very inception, voted Conservative saw Tory candidates elected post-2015. Former mining towns in Derbyshire, Staffordshire and Northumbria turning blue. Similarly, and at the same time, seats that had never voted Labour, like Kensington and Chelsea, Canterbury, Mid Bedfordshire, were turning red. Brexit divisions, geographical demographic shifts, fracturing of class boundaries in a post-industrialised service economy saw old tribal loyalties mixing blue and red and turning everything an unpredictable brown colour.*

No amount of electioneering would work on me – I vote Labour. In 2010 I threatened not to, and for the life of me I cannot now remember why I was so annoyed. If I could have 2010 standards of politics and services back, I would. As I walked out of the polling station having cast my vote, my husband said, 'Did you get your hissy fit out of your system or did you just do what was inevitable and

---

* I realise blue and red makes purple, I remember reception-class science, that and learning that a peanut would burn because it had fuel in it. Some things never leave you, but purple is the colour of the Brexit Party/UKIP/Reform or whatever the hell they are calling themselves this week, and frankly I think that a political party that has basically never in a general election won a seat in the House of Commons gets far too much attention and I, for one, am not joining in with the fawning! So, let's stick with brown because that's what you'd get if you mixed Labour, Tory, Lib Dem, Green, SNP, SDLP, UUP – a brown mess.

vote Labour?' He knew I was only capable of casting my ballot one way. In my defence, so annoyed was I that that very week I rejoined the Labour Party and was within the year selected to be the candidate for a local council seat and within the following year selected as the candidate for parliament, so at least I took on some responsibility to change things. Some hissy fit.

Tribal politics serves communities poorly, in my view, certainly in a local context. I think safe seats where x demographic of a community always votes Labour or y demographic always votes Tory means that the locals end up with a great representative who properly serves their area by luck alone. It does happen, but the levels of accountability within safe seats and tribal loyalties do not fit a model I would design. Perhaps it's my Northern Irish heritage and fascination with their politics that puts this into focus for me. Tribal loyalties there have for several years delivered no political leadership at all, with a non-functioning administration ending up ruled almost wholly by Westminster. Politicians must be kept on their toes at all times by their electorate and if they can phone it in on the basis of ancient religious, race, class or wealth factors then frankly they are more likely to end up doing a shit job than not.

So, the electioneering of Jeremy Hunt's stupid inheritance tax announcements is not for my benefit. It is for the illusive floating voter. The sensible non-tribal sorts who don't vote on the basis that their long-dead grandad is watching over them in the polling booth wielding a ghostly hammer and sickle. Why is it that just operating good sensible government isn't enough? If that was all it took to win elections, surely those who desire power as much as many in Westminster do would just focus on that. Why don't they?

I have taken some blame for the stupidity of my tribal tendencies, now so too must you. The average voter, you are part of the problem. Far be it from me to slag off voters. Professionally speaking, it is a silly and hazardous thing to do, but hear me out. You are never satisfied. I blame myself; people like me have gobbed on and on about how people should stand up and speak out. I stand by this, but when I think of Sharon Storer standing outside the Queen Elizabeth Hospital valiantly haranguing Tony Blair and demanding better treatment for her partner in A&E, perhaps it is hindsight that allows me to say, 'Be careful what you wish for, bab.'

I think she was absolutely right to take the opportunity when presented to her of expressing her displeasure. I don't think she should bow down to the prime minister as if he was some godlike person who should be respected no matter what. He is there to serve her, not the other way around, and she was simply fighting for better for her partner, which I have absolutely no doubt she received after the media attention her complaints garnered.

However, the overall effect was not to improve the health service for the future; it was merely a punch-up during an election campaign that Tony Blair's opponents will have been delighted by. The likeliest outcome of such an encounter is for politicians to stage-manage all visits to hospitals and schools, to the point where they will become incapable of actually seeing any sense of the reality on the ground. If Rishi Sunak had walked into the A&E waiting room where I sat that winter he would have, I suspect, struggled to make it out alive.

Elections bring out the Punch and Judy in everything, including the public, and become solely about who can hit the other person over the head with a truncheon more successfully. There is literally no light, no diligent plans for a better service, no acceptance of the difficulties of delivery or lengthy thoughtful conversations about the why and how things need to be better.

I love elections and the thrill of the campaign, but the election cycle merely breeds a culture of repeated actions: at most a year of planning followed by a year of set-up, a subsequent year of delivery then everyone loses their marbles again and starts shouting and screaming about how the other side have blood on their hands.

It would be wrong of me not to point out here that in my experience of election campaigns they are, on the national stage, by and large run by men. I am being polite by calling them men, because the way they actually appear to me is as boys. Boys pretending that they are in *The West Wing* – my God, does the Josh Lyman character in the Aaron Sorkin drama have a lot to answer for in what is wrong with our politics. Gangs of boys with made-up job titles poring over laptops and cracking witty jokes thinking that they run the fucking country have become a staple in Westminster politics of the last twenty years.

This is not an insignificant problem in how democracy plays out. In every political party HQ today there sits a nerve centre of boys acting as if they are fighting an actual war. Cosplaying tough talk and using the language of traps and ambush like they are the Rebel Alliance trying to fell the Death Star. Many of these people on all sides are certainly brilliant statisticians, great writers, brilliant communicators, but the number of fucks they give about actual public services being delivered satisfactorily is zero. They are often either too young or too rich to worry, and their maleness, even for the ones with children or sick parents, means they are likely delegating their interactions with the state to a wife, sister or mother. They all live in London, even the ones who, like Dominic Cummings, came to their jobs with the lilt of a regional accent.

There have of course been some notable exceptions to this. I think of the brilliant Margaret McDonagh, Labour Party organiser and campaigns chief in the 1997 and 2001 elections, who definitely made those campaigns feel as if they were about public service delivery. But the point stands, I'm afraid: part of the reason we are poorly served in campaigns is because there is a distinct smell of Lynx Africa emitting from the room where we work on messaging. I guarantee you that the people briefing Jeremy Hunt's inheritance tax nonsense were a bunch of lads. The same week the very same boys were briefing the following: 'Exclusive: Downing Street officials are looking at changing the government's fiscal rules in an attempt to set a trap for Labour over borrowing.' Like they are not even embarrassed that they are plainly saying that government officials – paid for by you, the taxpayer – who should be working hard in your service on the issues facing the nation, are fannying about in the seat of power trying to lay traps. For fuck's sake, at least pretend you are doing the job you are paid to do, not just playing some revolting game of one-upmanship. My response to this 'Exclusive' tweeted out by the *Telegraph* was: 'Seriously, could they spend one minute actually trying to govern the country. Last week I had to put on a hospital gown in a toilet in a hospital, as there were no cubicles free from people, and the floor was covered in piss. Seriously, do your goddamn job.' I stand by this.

In the battle to be the victor in our democracy, hitting hardest always triumphs when you pretend it is a war you are fighting rather than a country you are governing. No one wins, you understand, just who sheds the most blood is the metric for success.

My solution to this particular problem is a simple one. Employ and elect more women from diverse backgrounds. It's an evergreen statement. Assume I think it about everything.

The solution to the wider problem thrown up by election cycles and the brutish black-versus-white system we have created is trickier for sure.

But we cannot be distracted anymore by cynical, negative tactics. While Twitter battled over fictional inheritance tax policy the next day, people sat for far too long in crumbling NHS waiting rooms up and down the country.

We deserve better. But to get it, we have to demand better. We cannot fall for it any longer. There are actual lives at stake.

2

Culture Wars

'The internet is leaking on you again.'

This is a phrase I have tried to remember ever since I first heard it uttered by my husband, Tom. Let me set the scene for you. It's a sunny Saturday afternoon. My husband and I are sitting in our back garden with my brother, who works at a university in the study and service of drug rehabilitation, and my sister-in-law, who is a children's social worker. Chatting about various things in the way families do, taking the mick out of each other, rolling our eyes, you know the drill. The conversation arrived at a story about trigger warnings. Before I go any further, I would like to issue you with a trigger warning that some of the things I am about to recount are not very polite about trigger warnings.

My brother was bemoaning the fact that sometimes it can take an age before getting going with anything at the university where he works because of the need to outline all of the possible content that may be alarming. He was describing some training he'd been in run by an external provider and said that about the first twenty minutes of an hour-long session was used to discuss how people might feel about the content. My sister-in-law said how in her social work degree this had been pretty common too; however, in practice there wasn't really much of that going on, she was relieved to say. I guess anyone in children's social work who required a twenty-minute trigger warning each day would very probably not have gone into children's social work.

They were both dismayed at how ridiculous it was, specifically how frequent it had become in academic settings and how tedious it made their learning and working environments. It was some absolutely classic case of older generation (they are both in their forties) bemoaning the preciousness of the younger generation. Every generation does it, it's not new, but for some reason the prevailing manifestation of the older generation tut-tutting at the youth seems to feel it has primacy in its criticism. It doesn't. As I say, this has always been the case. My grandparents' generation bemoaned my parents' generation for being soft hippies who didn't know they were born; my parents did the same to my brothers and me; now that we are the parents we are simply doing the same. 'This generation won't trouble the statue makers' is an idea that goes way back. It's just that my grandma didn't have the internet, so she was only annoyed within the confines of her own home about the things she was actually exposed to day to day. At most she might have chatted disdainfully over the fence to Elsie next door.

I listened with amusement and some agreement to how

the situation had got out of hand and laughed at my brother's explanation. However, I then tried to defend trigger warnings. I have, after all, worked for decades with victims of sexual violence, child abuse and exploitation. I can see why someone who has suffered a horrific rape might want to know before they settle down to watch *Game of Thrones* with a bucket of popcorn that there are going to be scenes of sexual violence so they can make an informed choice not to watch it.

I remember when I first started watching the hit American TV show *Breaking Bad*, I got two episodes in and I found the storyline about a man dying of cancer and a wayward at-risk drug-addict teen, and the horrors that world brings, a little too close to home. I was at the time nursing my dying mother through her crippling and ultimately fatal cancer, while also living with the consequences of my brother's very risky and dangerous heroin, coke and crack addiction. I decided that I would not continue to watch it in my evenings off from caring for and worrying about vulnerable people, because I didn't actually want to see the hardest bits of my life in technicolour in the name of entertainment. (Don't worry, I watched it all after my mom died and it is what she would have wanted because she would hate for me to be behind on the zeitgeist.) I get it. I get that a little bit of warning can save you from an evening's viewing that might make you sad. Personally, I managed to come to this conclusion myself without the need for a trigger warning. My husband carried on watching it without me.

If I really think about the times in my life where I have actually been triggered into a painful past experience it is so much more severe than just feeling sad about it. It can be an actual out-of-body experience, usually stemming from deep-hidden instances of trauma that have gone unprocessed. I have only experienced this once in my life. I was at the Cheltenham Literature Festival; it was a crisp, cold October day and I had just walked out of the lovely green-room tent sitting proudly in the middle of a stunning Georgian terrace-lined park. It is a truly beautiful environment, the kind you would see in a big-budget period drama. I looked at my phone and noticed I had loads of messages pinging up, which for someone in my profession usually means some big political news event has occurred and colleagues and friends are getting in touch about it, and journalists are seeking comment. No matter how boring my life is, I always assume it's something I have done wrong, or some scandal that is about to ruin my life, so immediately my anxiety (which I am medicated for) spiked. It was a message from Cathy Newman from *Channel 4 News* that I saw first. She was asking me if I was okay, clearly assuming I had heard the news already, and was expressing how awful it was.

I didn't know what she was talking about so, as I walked feeling panicky through this park surrounded by hundreds of literary festival-goers, I opened the BBC News app to see: 'Conservative MP Sir David Amess stabbed multiple times in incident at constituency surgery.' In this moment I can remember nothing I did, as if time had stopped and my place in the world had changed. I was no longer in Cheltenham; I was transported to a tiled room in southern Spain. I could feel my friend Ruth sat next to me trying to make me drink the cup of tea she had made, while I sat staring blankly into space. I was back in the room where I was sitting when the news reached me that Jo Cox MP, my beautiful friend, had died from her injuries after a similar attack on the way into her constituency surgery in Batley and Spen. I wasn't screaming or crying, I was just blank, empty, cold. Shock is, I imagine, the medical explanation.

Processing the sudden murder of a loved one is not something you usually have a frame of reference to lean on. I guess, in this instant of hearing about David Amess, the only reference point I had to protect myself was the moment I heard that Jo had died. I wasn't transported back to when I heard she was attacked; it was the exact moment I received the message from a friend that she had died that I returned to. It was my body trying to prepare me for the worst. Clever body. I've no idea how long I quantum-leaped back to that moment; it felt so utterly real to me that when I awoke from it, I was on a bench in Cheltenham I had no recollection of sitting on and I was shocked that my friend Ruth was no longer sat next to me. This is what actually being triggered means, it is a real phenomenon. No warning could have stopped it, and I am not sure I'd have been better off not to feel it. It did alert me to the fact that I probably needed to deal more thoroughly with initial trauma. Like I said – clever body.

However, my defence of the trigger warning to my

brother and sister-in-law was a hard sell, because there are not too many people who have suffered more trauma than the two of them in both adulthood and childhood. My brother, as I've said, was very ill with drug addiction and mental health problems, such as drug-induced psychosis, for decades. He has suffered abuse and violence that I actually largely don't really want to think about, including sexual abuse. My sister-in-law was a child refugee; her biological father was in prison for most of her childhood and she has suffered a series of dreadful and painful relationships, including the years of my brother's drug addiction. She is now living with terminal cancer. Rather than wanting to switch off from these experiences, they have dedicated their working lives to supporting others in similar situations to the ones that hurt them so very badly. If they were to receive trigger warnings in their working lives about things that might cause painful memories to them then they would literally get nothing done.

My brother went to university late in life and was a mature student. I remember the mature students from when I was studying for my undergraduate degree. I hate myself for saying it now because it makes me seem like a prick, but I found them to be exceptionally tedious, always referencing their life experience in debates about social policy. 'Yeah, Susie, we get it. You're a single mum and have an opinion in a debate about benefits for single parents, but unless it's on the reading list, can you just not explain this in every single lecture.' I really only disliked them because they were actually grateful and keen to be at university, whereas I was merely tolerating it as the expectation of a girl like me who turned eighteen under the Blair government, which pretty much aspired for everyone and their wife to go to university. I had no real aspiration or drive to be there, and the presence of someone who had positively chosen it, at some financial risk, and was going to make the most of it was to my teenage eyes just a massive try-hard.

My brother, I imagine, presented the same to many of those he studied and still studies with. He was a 40-year-old reformed drug addict, the father of two young sons, and he got a bloody first-class honours degree. Massive try-hard. The point that he made pretty deftly was that the trigger warnings were intended for people like him, people who had suffered immense trauma, but instead he felt that they were being used either for some sort of performance or out of fear that a student would complain should they not be in place and someone found the content difficult. He asserted that no one had ever once asked him if he actually needed warning about such things. He maintains that he doesn't. He is also not suggesting that some of the content doesn't make him feel sad and upset about some of his life experiences and the choices he made, it does, but he's okay with that.

It seemed to me that far from being bothered by the idea of a trigger warning, if it was dealt with briefly by just a quick overview of what was to be discussed he wouldn't think it at all noteworthy. It was the fact that the warning seemed to be pandering not to him as one of the only people in the room who had real-life experiences of the very thing that was about to be touched on, but to the younger students in the room, whom he perceives as being so desperate to be offended or victimised by stuff that the university had to cover its back by wasting everyone's time.

It was my husband who levelled the argument between us, by simply saying, 'The internet is leaking all over you all.' He told us that never once in his working or personal life had he ever heard people talking about, expecting or being disappointed by a trigger warning. He said he only knew what the term was because he'd heard comedians making gags about trigger warnings. He said that outside of Twitter and academia, trigger warnings were not a thing that happened or that anyone gave a toss about.

He was not defending the position of anyone else in the conversation; he thought we were all mad for caring about it at all. He was exasperated that three grown adults with busy lives and lots of responsibilities would choose to sit around in the garden on a sunny day whingeing on about trigger warnings.

His philosophy, as with so many things in life, is a simple shrug and no strong feelings about 90 per cent of the stuff we have been led to believe is absolutely tearing our country and our world apart. To him, the idea that, on a rare sunny day with our family while the kids ran around in the sprinkler, we would spend time fretting about trigger warnings – both for and against – was utter madness. He told us that we didn't really care one way or the other and that our annoyance or defence was completely confected, an invention of a fight that actually we all as decent humans could totally see both sides of and with a bit of common bloody sense. He sighed at us, disappointed by our stupidity, and told us this issue was not an issue at all. Not even a tiny bit. He concluded that the internet world and the world of university debates which we three partake in, and he doesn't, has turned us into time-wasting loons. He doesn't know that you can't say loons anymore, but like a slightly dated grandad you can't blame him, he's not on Twitter.

He's right, isn't he? Try to think of an issue that you have recently been incensed by. There are so many to choose from: trans rights, the teaching of critical race theory in British schools, Meghan Markle, Piers Morgan, what we should call Midget Gems. The list is endless. Is there a single one of these issues or fights that can't be improved by a completely common-sense approach that doesn't get annoyed? In almost 99 per cent of cases most people had no strong feelings about all the stuff we then go on to be really annoyed about because some twat on the internet has taken it too far. The fight is confected. My brother doesn't give a shit one way or the other about trigger warnings in reality; I don't either. I think that there is a chance that instead of always searching for strong feelings about stuff, we might need to step back and lean right into the fact that we have no strong feelings about most things. I think sensible solutions can be found in the no-strong-feelings zone.

At every book or political event I have spoken at in the last five years a question has come from the audience about how divisive our politics and our country have become; usually there is some nod to the effects of social media and the gross amount of trolling that I have personally suffered. Now, politics has become divisive, dangerously so – I refer you back to the time I was actually triggered. However, I do have to push back on this idea that the UK is in the midst of a constant battle in real life. I always ask the questioner whether, on the way to this particular event, they noticed anyone in the street having a row about defacing statues. Did anyone approach them as they bought their lunch in the Tesco Express and start judging their choice of ham sandwich as offensive to Muslims? Did anyone tut at them for wearing leather shoes, or throw orange paint over them and their petrol car when they arrived at the event? Of course they didn't. In real life people are cracking on, they like and dislike things, find some things problematic and others a delight without even a flicker of vitriol. I remind them that while it is a problem that in a single night hundreds of people can gather together online to joke about whether they would or would not rape me, not one person had that day shouted that I was thick, fat or unrapable. For the most part they had smiled, ignored me or done that halfway thing that people do when they come across the mildly famous – given me a quizzical look as if they couldn't place me and were trying to remember if I had worked with them in the past or served them recently in a Starbucks.

Now, true to the philosophy of Tom Phillips, I try to recognise when the internet is leaking on my real life.

My husband, while drunk with some of his mates, once tried to instigate the religion of Tom. He is a fan of L. Ron Hubbard's sci-fi canon and thinks it hilarious that he founded the religion of scientology, so thought he would give it a go himself. So far, the religion of Tom has only two disciples: our mate Mike, who is a kindly agreeable bloke who was happy to agree to anything, and our old lodger Matt, who is merely bucking against his Southern Baptist upbringing in Atlanta, Georgia. Everyone starts somewhere, I guess. However, I do believe my husband's philosophy could actually save us all from eternal damnation and the living hell of getting really cross about stuff some twat said on the internet, so he may be on to something. Most people have absolutely no strong feelings about all the stuff we are being told we have to constantly fight about.

The internet has well and truly leaked all over politics. Westminster fucking reeks of the shit. Here it is not merely confected arguments started online, the leakage has been honed into culture war dividing lines that people seek to use for political advantage. It is entirely in the gift of you, the reader, to allow this or to stop it.

There are almost too many ridiculous examples for me to outline them all, but I will try. Let's deal with the trivial first. On a perfectly normal day in Westminster, I descended the stairs of Portcullis House, the building that houses MPs' private offices on the Westminster estate, to grab myself and my staff a cup of coffee from the vendor in the large atrium where people sit around to chat. The coffee shop is called the Despatch Box, a nod, in the newer part of the parliamentary estate, to the ancient traditions of our democracy. The despatch box being, of course, the boxes in the main chamber that the prime minister and the leader of the opposition lean on during Prime Minister's Questions. The Despatch Box coffee shop is an unremarkable caffeine outlet; however, I will remark that the coffee is dreadful. After I had been served at the counter, I took my flat white over to the station provided to administer sugar and milk to sweeten my no doubt tasteless brew. Next to me stood an older Conservative MP who was performing the same mundane task. He asked me to pass him the milk jug, and then said in pointed jest, 'Oh, am I allowed to ask you to pass the milk these days when men have to be careful what they say to women?' The barb was, I assumed, aimed specifically at me as a feminist and as one of the people who had campaigned in the House of Commons for processes and practices to be put in place to change the culture of bullying and sexual harassment. Such a spoilsport that I don't think government ministers getting a bit handsy with their researchers should be ignored. One of the most hated things that was proposed – incidentally not by me, but who cares about facts these days? – was mandatory training for all MPs on bullying and harassment. Many took real umbrage at the suggestion that they would need training, considerably more umbrage than they took at the fact that loads of young men and women had come forward to speak about being groped, abused and exploited by MPs. I simply responded, 'Oh, you can ask me to pass you the milk, just don't grab my tits while you do it, it's not rocket science.' He looked horrified and I assume he thought me as tasteless as the coffee. You see, only some people are allowed to deliver barbed gags. Apologies if my barbs are better than yours.

I have heard several variations on this in parliament, where some of the men there have quite simply lost their minds in the debate about the treatment of women at work. The saying 'equality seems like tyranny if you have been privileged' comes to mind, but their distaste almost exactly mirrors the nonsense spouted online about women making up allegations and men being so marginalised – I believe the term is 'cucked' – by women as to not be able to be men anymore. What a dreadful view of mankind it is to say that if men can't be bawdy, sexist and sexualised at all times their very existence is threatened. Why do people who assert this hate men so much and think them so pathetic? So much nonsense gets spouted about how 'you just can't say anything anymore', especially about interactions with women.

Now this fella getting his coffee was just making a joke, I was not mortally wounded by it. It gave me no cause for complaint to anyone, I was not upset. Just, if he is going to dish out jokes, I'd suggest he also learns to take them. Other men in parliament, I note with some glee, have chosen an-other tack in response to the #MeToo movement, instead of trying simply to be against it for the sake of a row or even a gag. I remember Tory MP Dominic Grieve before he left parliament in 2019 chatting with me in the tearoom as we queued together to get a cuppa. He said to me, 'I really hope this isn't inappropriate to say, but your new haircut really suits you and you look remarkably well recently.' Do you know what, lads, I really, really don't mind you commenting on my looks if you are not a massive dick about it. I can imagine Mr Grieve would have had the exact same comment to make about a male colleague who perhaps had started to sport a flattering beard, or who had lost a bit of weight. He wouldn't have led his comment to any of them with a worry about whether or not it was inappropriate, because it could never possibly be construed as such. But in doing so to me he recognised that for all my life, and the life of all women, comments about our appearance have been a hindrance or a trial for us. I appreciated the prologue, it made me feel seen.

Darren Jones, the Labour MP for Bristol North West, on seeing me the day I returned to Westminster having lost my mother-in-law to a sudden heart attack, approached me to ask how I was. When he saw that I was a bit shaky and not my usual sweary, give-no-shits self, he asked me if he could give me a hug. He asked my permission before touching me. There are other men, such as Wes Streeting, Pete Kyle and Chris Elmore, who I have a very familiar relationship with, we hug each other all the time, so they would never need to ask. Darren and I are very good friends but are not like that. I found it utterly moving that he asked me. It was in no way awkward as he embraced me and it made me feel not just loved and cared for in my bereavement but also understood as a woman for whom vulnerability has, in my life, been a dangerous beacon for bad men to exploit. Of course, he didn't think that deeply about it when he asked, but the fact he thought about it at all was enough.

You see, adults acting with complete common sense can wander through complex issues that are highly charged and have bear pits to fall in without any trouble at all. To suggest you don't know where the appropriate lines are in normal human behaviour because of a confected fight you have seen on Twitter is a terrible admission for any adult human; for one who claims to be in touch and represent people, I'd say it means you are fundamentally unfit for the job. It is not a brag that you just don't know how to talk to half the population anymore, it's an embarrassment. Don't do it.

But some MPs talk about nothing but culture wars. They are known for nothing but being angry and 'bravely' daring to say the unsayable. I guess if you have never changed a single law, never made a decent speech, never been good on the telly or been called on for your in-depth knowledge on a particular policy area then the only way to make your mark in modern politics is to act like a complete dickhead. It's tempting to ignore it or to dismiss it as trivial in order to get through the day. But in truth it is quite dangerous because it contributes to the febrile arguments online that make political activism so unbearable for people, and it also makes politicians as a class look terrible, as if we don't care about the real issues in the country, like NHS waiting lists or our diminished armed forces.

There are plenty of examples I could cite – literally look up anything that Jonathan Gullis or Lee Anderson says. It is entirely designed to make you cross. They know what they are doing when they moan about having to say police officer rather than policeman or woman, or when they slag off people who use food banks. The clicks and the vitriol are the goal. When they claim to be speaking for the ordinary British person too afraid to speak up, they are literally begging for you to respond, 'Well, you don't speak for me.' See also Nigel Farage's entire career. Don't give them what they want, just laugh at them quietly in your living room and move on with your day. I will concede that you should, if you live in their constituencies, write to them. Don't bother taking on the nonsense they have spouted, just tell them that as one of their voters you are a bit embarrassed by them, and that maybe they could focus on people who really are too afraid to speak up, like workers silenced by aggressive employers, women trafficked into sexual exploitation or postmasters wrongly accused of being crooks. Just a thought. Also, do respond to them if your comeback is so witty as to actually leave a thorn in their side. The bar for this is incredibly high; frankly, if you are not at Marina Hyde levels of political sketch writing this is a dangerous pursuit.

The example I think best sums up how badly the internet is leaking on Westminster is that of Nick Fletcher MP. Never heard of him, right?* He is a political nonentity. Since he won his seat in 2019, I have been in parliament

---

* Genuinely, as I wrote this, I had to Google him, using the search words of his stupidest moment because I couldn't remember his name. I wrongly wrote it at first as Nick Herbert MP, who I would have mistakenly besmirched. Nick Herbert seems, from a quick search, to be a perfectly normal MP who didn't make statements just for clicks. I did, however, find a newspaper article about how Suella Braverman wanted to remove him as the chair of the College of Policing because of his woke beliefs, so I guess that makes my point too.

with him for over four years and I have no idea what the pressing concerns of his constituents are or what policy area was the burning passion that brought him to the Commons. This is not necessarily all his fault, perhaps I could have paid more attention – and there are a lot of MPs. But to be fair, I do know what lots of them care about; it is hard to avoid as a Member of Parliament even if the public seem to manage it pretty well. I know Tracey Crouch really cares about sport equality; I know that David Davis obsesses about civil liberties; I know that Mark Spencer is big on farming – these are not debates I am involved with particularly, not much farming in Birmingham Yardley (we did have a cow in Sheldon Country Park for a spell and one of the schools has a llama, but as far as livestock goes it's not an issue I see a lot). You get to know because they bring it up all the time, invite you to events about it, enlist your support for debates on the matter. I don't mean to blow my own trumpet, but I am not sure anyone who had ever heard of me would be in any doubt about what I went into politics to change. If there is an MP who doesn't know that I campaign about men's violence against women and children, then I assume they are dead. I don't hide it. Nick Fletcher is a question mark.

I can only assume that it is his very meh-ness that has led him to try to stand out by saying utterly ridiculous things. Chief among his nonsense, and what catapulted him to the headlines and any kind of public consciousness, was his statement that 'there seems to be a call from a tiny, yet very vocal minority, that every male character or good role model must have a female replacement. One only needs to look at the discussions surrounding who will play the next James Bond. And it's not just James Bond. In recent years, we have seen Doctor Who, Ghostbusters, Luke Skywalker, the Equalizer, all replaced by women, and men are left with the Krays and Tommy Shelby. Is there any wonder we are seeing so many young men committing crime?' In this statement our mate Nick seemed to be saying that the reason men commit violent crime is because Doctor Who was at the time being played by a woman. He claimed afterwards that he was merely trying to say that men need good role models just as women do, which seems odd to be leaning on James Bond as a good role model. I guess if you want your men to grow up married to their job, constantly committing violence, and to have a questionable relationship with women, then, yeah, Bond is a cracker.

Obviously, when the Ghostbusters were all played by men there was much less violent crime committed by men, and presumably fewer angry male ghosts. When Doctor Who was played for the last fifty years by a man, women went delightfully unmolested, it would seem. Also, mate, Luke Skywalker is still very much played by Mark Hamill, who is very much still a man. As for the Krays and Tommy Shelby now being the only role models available to men and boys, I might suggest that Nick Fletcher maybe changes the channel – there are definitely still plenty of dudes on the telly box being loving fathers, swashbucklers and inspirational leaders. Men don't just look at Tommy Shelby from *Peaky Blinders* and think, *My God, crime looks fun*. Funnily enough, in the series (spoiler alert) Tommy Shelby goes on to become a Birmingham Member of Parliament and I can assure Nick Fletcher that, as the only Birmingham MP to be depicted in a drama for me, a Birmingham MP, to look to as a role model, I have never killed anyone in a gangland shooting. Or, might I add, been involved in *any* killing. I guess I have been stopped in so doing because Queen Latifah took over from Denzel Washington in *The Equalizer* (by the way, whether man or woman, the role is called on to commit immense yet apparently morally justified violence and torture). Even if he was misconstrued in the headlines, he surely knew what would come about from his nonsense – attention.

I don't mind what Nick Fletcher is saying; I don't disagree that men need good role models in life and on the telly. What I do mind is that Nick Fletcher is doing naff all to work on the woes of young men who turn to violence. I may have missed it, but on budget day I have never heard him calling for much-needed funding for now non-existent youth work provision. What efforts has he made to set up local youth services in his constituency aimed at young men? Where are the debates in which he has joined with campaigners like Roman Kemp to insist on mental health provision in every school to stem the tide of young men dying by suicide? I assume, as I do with vulnerable abuse victims, both men and women, that he has set up specific surgeries in his office to support the individuals and to research exactly what is going on in their difficult lives. Or is he just saying that we should have a Minister for Men (fine, whatever, knock yourselves out) and a men's health strategy? If you want a men's health strategy, Nick, and the government won't do it, (a) get a better government or (b) get writing. Come on, Nick, convene a group of experts in the field, meet with groups of men affected and put pen to paper. That's what I do when something I want doesn't exist, I invent it and eventually the government gives in because I am a pain in the arse. Crack on, mate, I will even help you to do it, because I am nice like that, probably because I had such a good role model as a child in Aunt Sally from *Worzel Gummidge*.

Maybe he meant to grab headlines with his nonsense, maybe he genuinely didn't realise that his comments would have been reported as such. However, once he got a taste for causing a stir on culture war issues, they became too delicious for him to resist going forward. When you are unremarkable, I guess there is nowhere else to go to get remarked upon. He has banged on about how women's rights are at risk from trans rights, but he did it in the same month as saying the following about women in a debate about abortion: 'Can we just think of those unborn babies and of the women having those abortions? Maybe, if they had used contraception or had looked at things in a different way, these babies would not have happened.' Oh, fuck off, mate. I can only assume he has never had sex because he seems to think that babies can be born only of woman. It takes two to tango, flower – maybe if all the men had used contraception it wouldn't have happened. He ain't no feminist; he just knows that trans rights and abortion rights get a lot of traction on social media, so he is like a rat up a drainpipe to give us the benefit of his wisdom on women's rights in debates on these topics. Plenty of MPs I vehemently disagree with on the issues of abortion, trans rights, race equality and other subjects can manage to speak in debates with complete common sense, care and caution so as not to cause a stir. There are no no-go issues; there are idiots who want to stir the pot.

I suspect, feeling that he was not getting enough attention, Nick Fletcher decided to claim that A&E waiting lists in his constituency of Don Valley were too long due to high levels of immigration. He said: 'We are turning parts of our community into a ghetto . . . you have to go to A&E and you get a twelve-hour waiting list, and the reason why the waiting list is so long is because people don't speak English in these places anymore.' It was later pointed out quite clearly in various newspapers that 94 per cent of the population of Don Valley were born in the UK and English is the mother tongue of 97 per cent of its inhabitants. I imagine, if my constituency is anything to go by, the other 3 per cent whose mother tongue is not English all work at the local hospital! Get rid of them at your peril, Nick.

The internet leaking all over parliament in the case of Nick Fletcher still sits very much in the trivial column of why this is a problem. Luckily, despite indulging in the worst machinations our country has ever seen, the Conservative Party recognises that Nick Fletcher is a no-mark, and he was never going to be troubling the cabinet table, so he has no real power or skills to actually get anything changed by his desire to spout nonsense for attention. What it does achieve, however, is to make politics itself look small and stupid. Journalists and Twitter thrive on this blather, so it gains far more traction outside of Westminster than it does inside. Radio phone-in shows will for days after such statements be dedicated to the nonsense, and people will be invited to row across the media and online about the issue in question. In Westminster it passes with an eye-roll and no further action. We still do not have a Minister for Men.* It makes people think that there is no point to a parliamentary democracy, when so much airtime is given to this bilge. Honestly, I cannot stress enough how small a dent the likes of Nick Fletcher have made on how laws are written or how the government operates. The attention given to these pathetic events just makes our parliament seem small, trivial and useless. Is it any wonder that young people living in the UK who are naturally more progressive are falling out of love with democracy?

What can *we* do to stop this tide of nonsense culture wars offering such lifeblood to idiots in Westminster? I am loath to say this because I do not for one second want

---

* Honestly, men, your message carriers for the idea of having a Minister for Men are really poor. If I had wanted this and had aggravated for it for as long as this has been doing the rounds, we would have one by now. We have a Domestic Abuse Commissioner, for example, which I banged on about, and the Labour Party at least has a Minister for Domestic Abuse and Safeguarding, even if the government just call it Safeguarding. If this is something you really want, do let me know and I'll crack on getting it for you because the eejits who ask are very easy for everyone to ignore.

some of the things that pound-shop Enoch Powells* say to go unchallenged, but we have got to start ignoring it. We must not let them get us all riled up to the point where we ourselves are living in a constant state of vexation. I know it seems counterintuitive, but I think we are drinking poison and expecting it to kill someone else. Be more Tom Phillips; we have to stop falling for the lie that these hot-button issues have any relevance in our actual lives. Twitter spats and political gaffes, no matter how offensive, do not actually affect our day-to-day lives even when they specifically target us and our identities. Nick Fletcher directly insulted me in his comments about abortion. I have had an abortion, not because I was too dumb or randy to use contraception† but because contraception failed me. What he said was deeply offensive to me but it doesn't in any way affect my life that he said it. Stupid people will always exist and had I entered into a full-scale row with him on the matter you might have heard of him.

The purveyors of this type of nonsense want a reaction, just as bullies do. They want people like my brother and me to sit around discussing them; it pulls us away from the very important work we both want to get on with of

---

* Enoch Powell is one of only two famous names who hail from my constituency. Can I say that we are all eternally grateful that Malala Yousafzai is the other one in order to provide some balance. One was a demagogue who hated immigrants, the other was an immigrant who fought so long and hard for girls' education in the face of near-fatal opposition that she won the Nobel Peace Prize. Thanks, Malala.

† I once asked a DUP MP who asserted that women use abortion as a contraceptive if he thought I had only had sex three times.

making the world a safer, fairer place. Also, it literally earns money for them and for Elon Musk. A handy tip to stop you from reacting is to imagine that you are handing Elon Musk a tenner for every sentence you write that joins in with the froth. He is writing computer code precisely to try to ensure you are at maximum ire. Why are you giving Elon Musk money to help him keep you unhappy and keep Laurence Fox in your life? Elon has enough, you don't need to help him anymore.

Culture war purveyors are having arguments with a cloud. Conservative politicians seem of late, led in no small part by neo-con super-mum Miriam Cates, to suggest that politics cannot mention the concept of family because it is met with the confected rage of liberals. What utter bloody rubbish! In failing to find any examples of politics being fearful of talking about family and families (it will happen at least one hundred times every single day that a politician speaks of or invokes the concept of family) they just say it is, if they are brave enough to do so. Miriam, bab, you are literally shouting at a cloud as it slowly wafts overhead; talk about the concept of family all you like, love.

A Tory minister, who picked up on the conspiracy idea from the internet of '15-minute cities', took to the airwaves stating that they would never allow people to be controlled by the state when it came to how far they could travel to a shop. Something literally no one had suggested. Mark Harper, the transport secretary, soiled himself while saying, 'What is sinister, and what we shouldn't tolerate, is the idea that local councils can decide how often you go to the shops, and that they can ration who uses the roads and when, and that they police it all with CCTV.' No council in the country is or was telling anyone how regularly they could go to the shops, because that would clearly be mental. Harper was standing on the stage at the Conservative conference while he had a row with this cloud. Point and laugh by all means, but if we start shouting at the person who is shouting at a cloud we also start to look mad.

My great-auntie Mary, who I used to help care for in my childhood, suffered latterly with some quite severe mental health problems; she had also gone blind and so felt very paranoid about what was happening that she couldn't see. She was absolutely convinced that Saddam Hussein was targeting her and, on one occasion, which I will admit at the time we were amused by, she thought he had sent someone to steal her knitting. Of course, she was unwell and deserved care and sympathy, but the level of credence we gave to her accusation is the same as we should give to these ridiculous invented bogeymen that politicians keep leaning on. No one is trying to ban going to the shops or even suggesting it, or telling politicians it is offensive to mention families, any more than an Iraqi dictator and killer of Kurds was pinching my auntie's half-made mittens from a bungalow in south Birmingham.

Yes, it is true that some people will believe the stuff they spout and so it presents a dangerous tone, but I really feel that we should have a little more faith in the British public and our country's journalistic mettle to point out, as they did with Harper's absolutely batshit claim, that that is all it is – batshit. Don't let them puppeteer you into such a froth that you end up breathing life into their dead cat until it is prowling all over your television studio.

I had to practise what I preach not long ago when culture war mouthpiece Katharine Birbalsingh, who is apparently the UK's strictest headteacher, decided I was this week's meal ticket. In a week when I assume she wasn't getting enough attention, she accused me of being a racist. Now, this was in some part my fault because I, while bored on a train if memory serves, responded (not directly) to something she had posted about Tina Turner (can I stress again how fucking trivial this all is). On the death of Tina Turner, she had posted a picture of Turner with known wife-beater and abusive husband Ike Turner and written 'Good times'. Twitter undoubtedly reacted with hostility to what, to me, seemed like clear baiting for attention. She claims it was a gif that had malfunctioned and stuck on that one image, whatever. I shouldn't have bothered reacting, it was a waste of my time, but I joined in and said it was offensive and that someone in charge of children should not have such an attitude towards domestic abuse. This woman is a chief culture war vulture, she loves to argue with clouds and had, not long before this incident, been speaking at an ultra-right-wing conference where her contributions of shouting at clouds had been widely reported. I should have lived by my own philosophy and just ignored her stupidity in posting about Tina Turner, be it benign or malign. Lesson learned; she is literally not worth my time and frankly she had featured so little in my life and in my anti-abuse activism that I didn't even know her name.

A few weeks later when she hadn't got quite enough attention again – I imagine the alt-right conference circuit had moved to another country, Hungary perhaps – she decided to restart the row by writing a public letter to my boss Keir Starmer in which she claimed that I, a lifelong domestic abuse campaigner, was offended by her posting of a famous domestic abuser and saying 'Good times' because I was a racist. She said of me: 'Her behaviour is a clear example of "unconscious bias". I mean that she hates me, despite not knowing me, because she subscribes to the idea that Black and Asian individuals in public life owe a duty to voice opinions that match with a left-wing view of the world, or they are worthy of her contempt.' Dear Katharine, I do not hate you, I literally couldn't remember your name when I tweeted about you because I rarely think of you unless I am laughing at you making a weird ranty speech. I am more upset by people sending me LinkedIn invites than I am by you; seriously, I dislike the robot who tells me there is an unidentified item in the bagging area more than I don't like you. You don't feature in my real life at all.

She used in her case against me a load of tweets that I had written, including one in which she claimed that I was suggesting that Asian Conservatives were not proper Asians if they were Conservative. This would, if I had said it, have been racist. Asian people can have whatever politics they want and, as someone who lives in an area with a huge number of Asian people, I know this – their politics is wildly varied, just, you know, like everyone else. The trouble was that the tweet she was referring to, which was from 2018 (some five years before the Tina Turner incident), actually said: 'The "I wanna be the leader of the Tories" charade that's been going on today is just the despicable, selfish, couldn't give a shit about the country I'd expect. The country is in a fucking crisis, you utter pointless parading peacocks. You ain't no Aslan.' She thought that I had said 'You ain't no Asian', which, given that I was referring to Boris Johnson and his behaviour in the 2018 Conservative leadership battle, would not have been inaccurate, he is not Asian. It would, however, have been a deeply weird thing to say. I was, of course, referring to the mythical lion from C. S. Lewis's *The Lion, the Witch and the Wardrobe*. I would like to apologise to fictional lion kings when I suggested that they were all noble leaders. Scar in *The Lion King*, for example, would not fit this mould and it was wrong of me to be so exclusive in my language. Never mind Ms Birbalsingh's views on domestic violence, both her ability to read and her basic comprehension seem a little shaky. Perhaps I, as a history scholar myself, might have some lessons to teach her about checking source material and ensuring it is not taken out of context. I feel my original point about her fitness to educate may have been proven.

The initial mistake on my part, of allowing myself to become angry, was made, so I now had to sign up to my husband's philosophy. While Ms Birbalsingh toured radio and television studios, I ignored it. I made no comment; I refused every single interview, both on my own and the many I was offered to go head to head with her. I just cracked on with my life and carried on doing my job as the Shadow Minister for Domestic Abuse and Safeguarding. She wanted me to have to go on telly and deny being a racist, which, no matter how much her mistaking Asian for Aslan made her look stupid, would still not be a good look for me. So, I didn't. A brilliant writer called Alex Andreou composed a Twitter thread that was a very detailed and completely dispassionate takedown of every single piece of evidence that Birbalsingh had cited in her letter to Keir Starmer. The lack of invective in this defence was what made it so cutting. I refused to bite and so she ran out of steam and the story just went away. She so desperately wanted me to react, to be mortally wounded by her vile attack, that I decided she didn't deserve my energy. When it all came out in the wash, few in my constituency were even aware this had happened. The only messages I got from my voters on the matter were in support of me. Funnily enough, especially from Black and Asian women who sent messages like, 'Is she having a laugh, ignore her!' Had I done what she wanted, the story would have been much bigger. I mean, I think I still would have won the substantive argument, because I can read, but she would have been the victor just by making space for nonsense.

So, I implore you, dear reader, to think twice before you reach for bile rather than humour in these instances. The desire is to make you cross until you are spitting feathers and start to look unhinged yourself. The aim of the game is to make people sit around in their gardens arguing about trigger warnings, rather than just politely going to see a course leader and saying, 'I think that there is a risk we might be wasting a bit too much of the time we have to discuss solutions in drug recovery on worrying about offending people – could we possibly just shorten that bit?' Yes, if someone is racist or sexist or homophobic it must be pointed out, but we have got to be very careful that we don't get pulled away from doing the actual work to stop it. I'll spend time being offended that someone refers to me as 'her indoors' when I have improved the nation's rape-charging rate. All in good time, my friends.

Stop and think, *Does this really matter?* Sometimes it absolutely will, but I guarantee you that 99 per cent of the time the only effect will be to make you feel good for one second and then miserable with the world. Laugh at these people and move on; they are mad, bad and desperate for succour. One of the very best responses to this clickbait vitriol I have ever seen was when anti-LGBT activists were protesting outside Birmingham schools about the teaching of tolerance of gay people. The protesters were doing everything to create online content for their YouTube hate channels. A local group of musicians decided to counter the angry protest by assembling a choir outside one school and singing songs about love, such as Louis Armstrong's 'What a Wonderful World', Judy Garland's 'Over the Rainbow', Labi Siffre's 'Something Inside So Strong', The Beatles' 'All You Need Is Love' and

Arthur Kent's 'Bring Me Sunshine'. Love and humour are the very best response.

So that's the trivial; the trouble is that the trivial has laid the stage for the downright sinister. This environment created by idiots, attention seekers, greedy algorithm purveyors and bad state actors has leaked on Westminster in a way that is far from trivial. Let me take you on a trip to Rwanda.

3

Rwanda

So culture wars, when practised by no-marks from the internet or MPs you've never heard of can be laughed at and ignored. Unfortunately for us, it's harder to overlook when pretty big players on the political stage, both here in the UK and around the world, get involved. This is where political lying created a culture that was toxic to public service, and that has real-world ramifications for a long time to come. This terrible bullshit of tiny-minded politics that thinks spiders are going to come and take over our schools and turn our children into rabid left-wing revolutionaries should have been laughed at by those in the country with real power. It makes our democracy seem thin-skinned and our great country appear to the rest of the world like Biff from *Back to the Future*. Thick, mean and angry. Not a Tinder profile you would swipe right on. But it wasn't; it was embraced with dangerous and expensive consequences that mean that, if you are a UK taxpayer, money is being taken out of your pocket as you read this. You are paying for Biff to bully.

I think it is probably worth going over the reasons why faceless avatars who use terms like 'native Brit' on sub-Reddit forums managed to pull up a chair at the cabinet table and grab a can of Coke in the bike shed around the back of parliament with incumbent prime minister, Rishi Sunak. When you are floundering in the delivery of basic public services, you need something to say that doesn't alert journalists or the voting public to the fact that you have crashed the economy, whacked taxes up to a seventy-year high, diminished the armed forces, and are presiding over a worrying trend in deaths from completely curable cancers.

You can always distract public attention by standing in front of a flag and shouting about how you love Britain and everything about it, even the legacy of slavery that should be remembered by old dudes made of marble on plinths. The culture wars give governments something they can make rallying cries to their base about. They couldn't fly flags* for lower taxes or free-market thinking when they hiked up taxes and gave out contracts to all their mates with zero competition at the same time as paying every-one's wages during Covid. They needed anti-progressive cultural views to keep them warm at night.

Politicians used to have the European Union to blame for whatever was wrong in our country, but they led us out of that so they are left looking around for old foes to blame for everything that is wrong in our country such

---

*   I really wish I had invested in flag manufacturing. It seems that the early years of this decade have been flag-heavy: Ukraine, Palestine, Israel, rainbow . . . there has been a lot of flag shenanigans in the UK.

as single mums, immigrants and the poor more generally. These have always been firm favourites for politicians to have a pop at. It's not the fault of those in Whitehall for not building enough houses over the last forty years; the reason you can't get a house is because poor, immigrant, feckless single mums have got them all. I still meet people every week who believe that immigrants to the UK get priority above them on the three-year-long waiting list for a council house. It is simply not true and, what is more, it would be illegal. Homeless people with a connection to the local area, victims of domestic violence, and veterans of our armed forces are the only groups protected in law for priority housing. I should add that it is in law alone, because most homeless victims of domestic violence I work with still wait around two years to get the keys to a council property and are left in heinous and unsafe temporary accommodation while they wait. Some priority! There is no place on the form for you to tick that says, 'Are you an immigrant?' which then magically gets you to the front of the queue. In fact, the opposite is true. In order to get on to a local council housing list you have to prove a local connection, so you have to have been resident or work in the area to qualify. Of course, many immigrants to the UK would qualify under these rules if, for example, they had moved to the area to work as a care worker. However, they would be given no priority on the list above a non-immigrant also with a local connection. I love the idea that local councils have a drawer full of keys to beautiful council houses labelled 'for priority immigrants'. They don't.

Facts, of course, do not matter in the culture wars. If it helps to distract you from record-breakingly bad house building over decades, or the selling-off and reselling of social housing without ever thinking to replace it, then so be it. Screw the facts, the falsehood is a way more powerful political tool.

The prevailing perception in the UK is that by far the majority of the migrants to our country are illegal immigrants who have come here on small boats across the Channel. When YouGov did a poll in early 2024, over 60 per cent said more migrants come illegally, while only 24 per cent of people polled thought it was the other way around. And 14 per cent said they didn't know, which, it turns out, was the case for far more of the people polled than they realised, because the reality is, of course, that irregular migrants made up only 7 per cent* of all migrants to the UK in the year 2023. Ninety-three per cent came completely legally to pick our daffodils, study in our universities and feed our infirm. I suspect if we tried to end all migration to the UK and it meant we couldn't all buy bunches of daffodils for a quid at every supermarket checkout, there would be genuine revolution in Middle England.

---

* In 2023, 672,000 legal migrants entered the UK; 52,530 were considered, in the year ending June 2023, to have entered irregularly. We cannot even say if they have entered illegally because their cases have not yet been assessed and they likely won't be for at least another year. Many will be found to have a completely legitimate claim for asylum, such as soldiers who fought with us in Afghanistan, or victims of modern slavery and trafficking, so in truth the percentage will be much lower. But they didn't come through one of the agreed routes, for example as students or to work in our farming and care sectors.

Why are people getting this so wrong? Politics, that's why. Politicians such as Suella Braverman and Rishi Sunak decided to try to stop people noticing that they had massively inflated the number of legal migrants to the UK post-Brexit, when they had promised (lied) that it would dramatically decrease. They had to find a flag to stand in front of to distract the people. The flag that they chose was people who arrive on small boats. The fact that your local library has closed is not the fault of years of austerity – nope, it's the fault of people on small boats. Called an ambulance lately and it didn't come? I'll tell you who is to blame, it's the small-boat folks. Your mortgage leaped from £1,000 to £2,000 a month? Not down to Liz Truss and her economy-busting lunacy – nope, it's those pesky small-boaters again.

I do not like that people arrive on small boats. Just to be clear, you would believe were you to listen to even the most sensible Conservative MPs as they become increasingly desperate to curry favour, that all Labour MPs want people to arrive on small boats. Some of the feverish comments I hear make it seem as if Keir Starmer himself is launching dinghies off the coast near Calais. Utter rubbish. I hate that poor, desperate people are being trafficked across dangerous seas in their attempt to seek a safe and secure future. I want it to stop, the Labour Party wants it to stop. It is cruel, expensive and unsustainable.

'Why don't they stay in France?' I hear every Tory cry. 'France is lovely, they have all that nice wine and cheese, what more do these people want?' Well, let me tell you a little story about some of the people I've met who arrived on small boats.

The very worst-ever period of my political career came at the time when the US and UK governments withdrew from Afghanistan, leaving the country to be taken over by the Taliban. I am not sure anything is ever going to compare to the desperation and workload in my office. I had thought prior to this that the first month of the Covid-19 lockdown had been difficult, when myself and my staff were trying to run logistics in a crazy new world to ensure our care homes were safe, our vulnerable people were fed, that children in the area had the technical capability to undertake home schooling. At the same time we were trying to allay fears about temporary morgues popping up in people's neighbourhoods, and for at least the first few weeks I was tracking local deaths and trying to reach out to bereaved families. It was an all-hands-on-deck situation and it was tough going. When you are ordering 'sorry for your loss' cards in bulk on the internet you can feel pretty despondent. This was nothing compared to the pressure my team felt when Afghanistan fell to the Taliban.

In 2021 when the US announced their hasty withdrawal from Afghanistan, overnight we realised just how many British Afghan people we represented. Thousands of people had settled in the UK, many of them in Birmingham, over the decades of turmoil in the region. As the evacuation of people from Afghanistan played out, my office became like a war room you might see in a disaster movie. Hundreds and hundreds of my constituents started to plead with us to help get their families out, most of whom had worked in some way for the UK or US governments, had fought alongside British soldiers, or, if they had no connection to Britain, were simply female relatives of my constituents who were about to face apartheid in the place they called home, banned from work, justice and education. What became clear as the situation unfolded was that news was spreading in Afghanistan among desperate people trying to evacuate that my office was picking up the phone and answering queries, and so we were flooded with enquiries that had no connection to Birmingham Yardley. How do you explain to desperate Afghans fleeing for their lives the parliamentary protocols that mean we can only take on cases linked to our constituents?

It was overwhelming how many cases we were taking on. We were initially telling people to send us images of their documentation and that we would seek to get them on the lists being compiled by the UK Foreign Office for evacuation, and then to make their way with their documentation to Kabul airport as safely as they could. This was the advice we'd eventually been given by the Foreign Office and so we dutifully followed it.

Many hundreds of images of people's passports flooded into my inbox, faces of men, women and children on their identity documents, many also sending pictures of themselves alongside British soldiers as proof, women sending pages of documents showing that they ran women's rights organisations. We were attempting to feed all of this information into the helplines and crisis emails that the government had set up, but it became pretty clear that there was a complete disconnect between those who were being let through onto the planes and those whose details we were submitting. We had the creeping sense hour by hour that we were literally sending all these details into a massive void, no feedback, no knowledge of who, if anyone, was reading it. In desperation, though, we just kept going.

It was chaos, and in the Zoom calls those MPs who were affected* had with the then foreign secretary, Dominic Raab (after he finally bothered to come back from his holiday), it was clear there was absolutely no grip on the situation. Staff from MPs' offices where the effects were the greatest quickly set up a WhatsApp group to share information and were devising together models for prioritising the cases among themselves. This was better than anything I saw Raab do in the time and, on one angsty Zoom call, I offered for my staff to take over the management of the records as it was clear, although not yet revealed in the press by a whistleblower, that no bugger was reading any of the stuff we were sending in. The *Guardian*, in reporting the evidence from the whistleblower Raphael Marshall, stated:

Marshall estimated that up to 150,000 people applied for evacuation, but that fewer than 5% of those got any assistance.

---

* This crisis obviously didn't affect all MPs equally; there are not too many British Afghans in the Welsh Valleys, for example. My caseload was the second-largest in the country and other MPs with one or two cases popping up were calling us for help with what to do, adding further pressure into the system.

He added: 'It is clear that some of those left behind have since been murdered by the Taliban.'

When a new system was introduced following fury at the masses of unread emails, Marshall said all emails were then read, but nothing was done with their contents and that he thought this was 'to allow the prime minister and the then foreign secretary to inform MPs that there were no unread emails'.

I will take a minute to praise the then defence secretary, Ben Wallace, who, in exasperation at the situation, just started giving out his personal mobile number to MPs like me with the biggest caseloads and linking us with the military personnel on the ground. The military personnel I communicated with both directly and indirectly were amazing and you could tell how frustrated they all felt too. Also, a massive shout-out to Lisa Nandy, the shadow foreign secretary at the time, who was desperately trying to push our cases. She and Ben Wallace together provided the only support I ever felt in a worsening situation.

My staff and I were on urgent calls to constituents on the ground in Afghanistan and also to the relatives of constituents. All we could say to them was to head to the airfield with their documents; we told them we believed but weren't sure that they would be expected. The worst moment came when, at the exact place we had been telling people to flee to with their children, a suicide bomb exploded killing 170.

In my memory this moment was almost cinematic,

although I imagine it wasn't in reality. The way I remember it, there was the ping of a news alert coming from someone's phone followed by Katherine in my office saying, 'Fuck, a bomb has gone off in Kabul', and we all just fell silent in horror and fear, before the silence was pierced by the sound of another phone call from a desperate Afghan.

It became pretty clear from the emails and calls we were receiving that travelling to the airport was becoming less and less safe and the Taliban were committing violence and aggression against those on their way there. My staff left their separate workstations and we huddled together in my office, put down our phones and tried to decide what we could do. It is in these moments that it falls to me and only me to make a decision. Most of the time my staff are perfectly capable of acting as the corporate body of Jess Phillips MP; they make decisions on cases and actions every day without needing to check with me. They know pretty well what I would do in a given situation and usually only call on me when cases are complex and if they need me to bollock someone. But there are some situations where the direction of travel has to be decided and, ultimately, I have to make that call. A week or so into this crisis, when my staff had worked sixteen-hour days, tracking and pushing cases from home and work, with constant communication between us all every waking hour, weekend or weekday, and holidays cancelled, events missed, I had to make the decision that we would stop advising people to travel to Kabul or around Kabul. We could no longer in good conscience try to get people out. Not only was it becoming increasingly unsafe, but it was also becoming futile. We were not succeeding. We were representing false hope. The systems we were relying on were failing us and the people we were trying to help. I had to make the call to stop.* In two weeks of effort to evacuate hundreds of people, in total my office managed to get just eight people on the planes. We helped others get out through Iran and Pakistan, and assured hundreds of others that we would keep trying to get them out through the future promised schemes that the government had alluded to that barely materialised. I wish I could tell you that had been a success but in fact we have managed to evacuate just a handful more this way.

The adrenaline you run on when you are in the thick of a crisis spurs you on. Also, the sense that you are doing a good thing, the buzz you get out of thinking that you are saving people's lives, is heady. I never once had to ask my staff to work extra hours: it happens organically; you roll up your sleeves and become a unit that is singularly focused on an outcome. You feel camaraderie and even delirium as events unfold and the moment you hear news that someone got out you explode into near-euphoric applause. This cannot be maintained; it is short and sharp and the crash and despondency of stopping, making the decision that you can do no more, the silence or the swearing that follows it, feels like a dark, cavernous void. You don't feel as if you

---

* If you were one of the people campaigning at the time to try to help the cats and dogs get out of Afghanistan and you were messaging my office with that campaign email at the very moment we were receiving the identity cards of children trying to flee, give your heads a wobble. The cats and dogs all got out.

tried and failed, you feel only as if you failed and, in this instance, failure meant death, starvation or enslavement. Big stakes. No matter how many times I congratulated my staff for their herculean efforts, even when in the following weeks those who got out of Afghanistan came into the office to embrace the familiar voices from the end of the phone who had helped them, the failure still fills the lion's share of the pit of their stomachs. I'm not sure I could ever ask them to do it again; their underpaid and at times heartbreaking job relies on progress made as currency. I wonder if Dominic Raab has ever lost the sleep that we did, thinking of those passport photo faces.

I do not love people coming to these sceptred isles by small boat, I hate it, but please forgive my glee when a lovely British Afghan man appeared at my office door unannounced, asking to be let in through the bulletproof vestibule. It was okay to let him in because we knew him; he came nearly every day during the fall of Afghanistan, pleading for us to help his brothers who were not safe because his father was a well-known army official who had worked hand-in-glove with the UK military. His brothers faced being murdered by the Taliban. We hadn't managed to get them out, and so this man would come in regularly over the following year asking if there was any progress in the various promised resettlement schemes. Letters to the ministers in charge, pushing the cases, all led to nothing. More and more as he came you could see his pride in his family's efforts with the British being tarnished by the silence and uselessness and, let's face it, cruelty of the UK government. But on this day as he walked in to see me, he was fizzing, almost hopping with excitement. 'They're here,' he said. 'They made it.' I threw my arms around him at the news, happy to see him not, for once, in angry desperation. 'How?' I asked, assuming I had missed an update in the case that my office had been diligently cracking away on. 'They came across the Channel.' His brothers had managed, through the efforts of some pretty amazing people on the ground in Afghanistan, most of them ex-British military, to escape through Pakistan and make it to France, where they had put their lives at risk and made it here to the UK. Why didn't they want to stay in France (remember all that cheese and wine)? Well, because their family is in the UK. They speak good English and no French and here in the UK, in Birmingham Yardley, they have a home they can live in, safe with their big brother who can support them. Also, they are Muslim, so the wine has little draw.

These young men, one of them a child when Afghanistan fell, should never have had to put their lives at risk in a small boat. Their family had risked huge amounts over the years to work with the UK government to build their country into a place where they felt safe. It was merely the luck of the draw, a life lottery in chaos and pandemonium poorly managed by the UK government, that they weren't already here.

These men are part of the 7 per cent of irregular migrants to the UK who the British public have been trained to hate in order to distract them from the government's failings. They only had to get on a small boat because of the incompetence of the UK government, because Dominic Raab was either too busy sunning himself in Greece or too fucking useless to manage any kind of referral system in a crisis. Suella Braverman, while in my city, wistfully dreamed of putting these men on a flight to Rwanda. It sticks in my craw that she said this at all; that she said it while in a room at the Conservative Party conference in Birmingham, where she was no doubt being served food and drink by people who had themselves been asylum seekers, is sickening.

The dream of sending these men to Rwanda was born entirely out of the Tory government's desire to have a row rather than an outcome. You, the taxpayer, forked out hundreds of millions of pounds of your hard-earned money because the internet leaked all over the government and they wanted headlines. In lieu of the European Union to blame for everything that is going wrong, they needed a different row.

They claimed that the Rwanda scheme would act as a deterrent and people would stop paying thousands of pounds to people smugglers to reach a better future, but there is absolutely no way that everyone who arrives irregularly in the UK could have been sent to the East African country. The details of the scheme were never clear at all because the government never told us how many people would go or how much it would cost, but at most it would have been a few hundred people each year. Being as fifty-odd thousand people arrived irregularly in 2023, how much of a deterrent is it that 1 per cent of those who come over on a small boat would be sent to Rwanda, when 99 per cent won't? When people make the decision to get onto a dinghy in dangerous seas where they might very well die, and more people have died than have been sent to Rwanda, why the hell would odds of 99 per cent in your favour act as a deterrent? There is no bet I wouldn't take with a 99 per cent chance of success. I have also never felt so desperate that I would step onto a crowded vessel that may cost me my life, but if I did ever face that prospect I'm thinking a 1 per cent chance of a flight to Africa isn't going to stop me when the risk of death didn't.

What is so galling about the small boats becoming a fight rather than a search for solutions is the things that the government didn't do to stop it while they spent years legislating and millions on legal fees to fight their case for Rwanda in the courts. It's the ultimate example of political lying getting out of hand. If they were really committed to this issue, why wasn't there more focus on law enforcement or intelligence gathering on the criminal gangs behind it? Now, this is a broad-brush statement; I know the National Crime Agency, who deal with organised crime in our country, have become pretty focused on the small-boats issue, and I am sure that this will bear some fruit. However, convictions of people smugglers dropped by more than a third between 2010 and 2024. In that time the government cut the budget for the NCA in real terms. But of course they did, why wouldn't they hollow out the agency that works on people smuggling?

As an inner-city MP in a diverse place, a lot of those who

are left trapped in our asylum system for years and years in hotel accommodation paid for again by you, the UK taxpayer, live in my constituency. I have on many occasions met people who have come over on small boats; they are mainly Afghan, Syrian and Eritrean. Usually, I meet them because they want me to chase the Home Office about their asylum application, which is taking years to process (oh, if only we had spent the £400 million we gave to Rwanda for nothing on processing cases). Every time I've met someone who came here on a small boat, I ask the same question: 'Has anyone interviewed you about how you arranged to be smuggled in?' The answer is always no.

On one occasion I asked this question of an 18-year-old lad who had come to the UK from Afghanistan. Like everyone else, he told me no one had ever asked him for any such details, and he looked a little worried that he'd missed some form he was meant to have completed. Now, I am the mother of an 18-year-old; for sure he has lived a different life to this young man, no doubt the Afghan teenager has had to take more responsibility for his actions and survival than my son, but the idea that an 18-year-old kid can find a smuggler (when my own son cannot find his shoes most days), and the UK law enforcement agencies can't, just beggars belief.

But before we embark on a scheme like Rwanda, why don't we start by interviewing, for intelligence, the people who arrive by small boat as a matter of course? For sure it is unlikely that many of them would feel able to speak, especially if they have been trafficked through violence and aggression and there is a threat to people back home. However, it cannot be beyond the wit of man to work out a supportive way for this intelligence to be garnered. They were all more than willing to talk to me, for example. I worked for years with victims of human trafficking who, despite suffering terrible trauma, gave up vital intelligence on organised crime. It's not rocket science; it's called being kind to someone. If you are more interested in headlines about being tough, and bragging about how you painted over a picture of Mickey Mouse in a children's asylum centre because it was too welcoming, perhaps you are doing a crap job. Hating these people and seeking to punish them is not working! For that reason alone, even if you don't care about the morality of it, you should maybe try a different tack. The definition of madness is doing the same thing and expecting a different result.

How is it that when Lewis Goodall from the News Agents podcast set about going over to Calais and investigating the smugglers he didn't find it very hard to locate the culprits and speak to them? I honestly may be missing something here, but I really cannot for the life of me assert that the Tory government did everything it could to stop this trade it claims to hate. I can therefore only conclude that the effort Rishi Sunak poured into talking about and fighting for the Rwanda scheme, meant the government were more interested in having red meat to fight about in the press than they were about actually solving the problem.

The failed Rwanda scheme is the very embodiment

of where the culture wars leaked out of the internet; it trickled over the no-marks, controversialists and idiots and seemed to gain some traction until it swelled into a tsunami that engulfed our government. The government wanted a wedge issue, they didn't care about the facts, the evidence, the cost to you; they wanted a quick and dirty slogan to put on the front of a lectern that would mean they didn't have to do any actual hard service-delivery work or efficiency management. They wanted a fight and a baddie to point at, they wanted the rowing and the vitriol, they wanted to divide and conquer, not to stop the boats, you see, but so that they would look tough and you, the voter, would like them.

They got the row, all right. It was rumoured in the papers that Rishi Sunak hated the Rwanda scheme when he was chancellor of the exchequer; he thought, accurately, that it was a waste of money. The home secretary at the time, James Cleverly, famously referred to the scheme as 'batshit'. So why persist? Because they liked talking about it. Because the plan to cause a row worked, even though they have not stopped the boats, and the only people who have been on a flight to Rwanda are various home secretaries carrying comedy big cheques in their luggage to hand over to an authoritarian government.* Their efforts would fail on literally every metric of service delivery,

---

* Paul Kagame, the president of Rwanda, must be an absolutely brilliant politician. In fact, he should write a book about how to do politics, because who could argue with a man so beloved by his people that he wins 99 per cent of the vote? Seems totally legit to me.

but they had a nice flag to wave. Someone else to blame for NHS waiting lists, housing shortages, violence on the streets – it's all the immigration, it's all those bastards on the boats, certainly not us and how we've managed the economy and public services since 2010. Nah, not that, it's the bloody boat people. Why bother to govern when you can wage culture wars instead? Feet up, tools down, let's just have a row. This is what needs to change. Think about the progress that could have made, with all that time, effort and manpower. Why did we put up with it? Which leads us neatly on to one of the very worst things about British politics: we have replaced doing things with just saying things.

4

Less Work, More Bullshit

Jess Phillips: Harvey, do you think that there is the capacity for police forces across the country to drug-test everybody who comes through their doors?

Harvey Redgrave: No, it needs to be attached to more resourcing.

JP: So if this law passes, it will not be able to be enacted?

HR: I am assuming there is an impact assessment and a cost that has been attached to the Bill.

JP: Never assume, Harvey. So currently, across the policing estate in our country, this would not be able to happen?

HR: I do not think it would be able to happen if you took current resource levels as the baseline. Some piloting is already going on in some forces, I think. I do not know how much of that has been allocated in future years.

This is a transcript of an exchange between myself and Harvey Redgrave, CEO of Crest Advisory, which is a specialist crime, policing and criminal justice organisation. The conversation took place in December 2023, during the line-by-line scrutiny of the government's proposed Criminal Justice Bill, in which they were trying to pass a law that everyone (where appropriate) taken into police custody on suspicion of a crime is tested for drugs.

You can have a long debate about why this might be worth doing. The bill calls for people in cases where substance misuse is found to be referred to specialist services for a mandatory appointment, which appears like a kindness unless you have any real knowledge of substance misuse services and how useless one single appointment that was forced on someone might be without the proper allocation of resource and service models with an evidence base. The negative of the policy is obviously that while drug-taking may have absolutely nothing to do with the crime you are suspected of – stealing nappies, say – you can bet your bottom dollar that if you had smoked a spliff three days before you nicked the nappies, that will be seen as a mark against your character and have an impact on your charging decision.

However, dear reader, I am not using this example to do a deep-dive into the pros and cons of our substance misuse systems being so inextricably linked with our criminal justice services.* Instead, I put this transcription in as an

---

* There is no war that has been so resoundingly lost as the war on drugs.

example of words not deeds. Whether you agree with the policy or not is, frankly, academic; it cannot happen. It is literally not possible. If you don't believe Harvey on this, I also asked Andy Marsh, a senior British police officer and CEO of the College of Policing, later in the same scrutiny session. Here's how that went:

Jess Phillips: Do you think that everything in the Bill could be implemented?

Andy Marsh: I am supportive of the measures in the Bill. Some will undoubtedly come with a requirement to increase the resource.

JP: Such as?

AM: The drugs testing would be a good example. I do not believe that there is currently a latent capacity waiting to do that.

JP: There is currently not the capacity available to do that?

AM: No.

JP: I didn't think there was. Okay, thank you.

Why, oh why, did I spend hours and hours in a poorly appointed committee room in the lofts of parliament debating a piece of legislation that would change absolutely nothing? I could have been spending that time doing something useful, like pairing socks or building furniture or, I don't know ... changing laws that will make the blindest bit of difference to the lives of the people in our country, or, as I call it, my actual job.

This case is a perfect example of how parliamentary politics has been simply about writing down words that mean absolutely nothing. The amount of people and time involved in the effort of writing down pointless words is phenomenal* when you consider the negligible effect those words then go on to have. Here, as I am writing words that will be published, so I will write down a new law – that everyone should get their birthday off work. Me writing this here makes it as likely to happen as if I had managed to get it written into a bill that then became an act – i.e., not likely at all. It is utterly maddening, which I think you can tell from this transcript. The only thing to do when faced with a piss-take is to take the piss back. The system is a joke.

The reason the clauses about drugs testing were put into this bill was for a headline, not an outcome. It was so the government could look tough on drugs, without actually doing the necessary work to make the policy happen or considering if it was in any way possible. No, that doesn't

---

* Parliament and government employ many people to write our legislation. The clerks who work on bills are seemingly completely invisible to the general public. I want to take a moment to praise a man called Kevin who works in the clerk's office. I worked with him on pretty much every amendment I have ever successfully made to the law, most importantly in the passage of the Domestic Abuse Act, but also on many others. You will never know this very understated man, but I would be so bold as to say that almost every piece of feminist legislation that we have snuck into bills in the last decade has been aided by Kevin's wise counsel. He is my parliamentary office's favourite person on the estate and we couldn't do our job without him. Let's hear it for the clerks.

matter, service delivery wasn't the aim; the aim was simply having something to say and write on a leaflet in an election year.

It would take, I imagine, longer than a decade for a policy like this to ever be realised. That's if, of course, like most things, it wasn't quietly scrapped in the next five years because of patchy roll-out, and because it would no doubt end up with some unfair treatment leading to scandal in one of the pilot areas that will be bunged some Home Office underspend to make it happen.

I would warn you to be incredibly sceptical of big numbers that get thrown around by ministers of state when they announce funding for something. Aside from big flagship policies such as the roll-out of Universal Credit, or Levelling Up (mind you, this was also utterly meaningless shit), ministers will often release pockets of funding for individual policies that they want to announce on a timetable of good news stories. The best examples I can give of this are in my field of expertise, on men's violence against women and children. At certain moments – like International Women's Day, or Valentine's Day, or during the UN sixteen days of action on violence against women and girls – the government always feels duty-bound to announce something. *Something* being the operative word: literally scrabbling around for anything to say on the matter. Seriously, try doing something every day, not just on the trendy days. Look out for it – on these days they will press-release something like the recent £2 million flee fund announced in the run-up to Valentine's Day 2024 to help give a few hundred quid to women who are destitute because of domestic abuse forcing them from their homes or work. Sounds good, right? Wrong!

I support the fund; there absolutely should be a government slush fund for victims of domestic abuse to dip into when they are facing real hardship. When I worked in Refuge there was always a tin of money that had been donated, which meant you could give out a tenner to a woman to feed her pre-payment meter and keep the lights on or buy nappies. I am not against the principle of the government taking part in what is essentially a state-level kitty jar. I am against them announcing it while touring news studios making out that it is a good news story and shows them to be brilliant and kind, when the reason most cited by women for their destitution in these dreadful circumstances is the delays built into the government's benefits system. It is literally government failure that leaves victims destitute. Yes, their perpetrator is to blame for them needing to flee, but the fact that the Tory government presided over police forces with falling numbers of charges for domestic abuse and rape, and built a benefits system that forces new claimants to wait six weeks after a change of circumstance for their first payment, is the goddamn problem.

The flee fund is nothing more than something to announce. It does no actual work or analysis on addressing the underlying systemic problems. It doesn't in any way shift government policy on benefits waits, and allows them to move on from the issue having stuck a plaster over the wound for a little longer. Two million quid sounds like a lot, doesn't it? Well, here is another problem with making announcements that sound good but hope you don't focus on the actual outcome while you feel grateful to our good and benevolent government. The fund can provide up to £2,500 to each victim assessed by the brilliant Women's Aid to receive it. So even if we went for a much lower figure, like £250 per victim, it will actually only help 8,000 victims of domestic abuse. Bear in mind that, in the year before the announcement was released, 10,000 women who had fled domestic abuse were found to have been refused accommodation support because it wasn't available. So even if we only gave it to these women currently fleeing and being left with nothing, 2,000 of them wouldn't even get £250 to tide them over. There are over 2 million victims of domestic abuse a year. On that metric the allocation is less than £1 each.

Numbers can tell a better story than the announcements themselves. The Criminal Justice Bill legislation also contains clauses about better monitoring of dangerous domestic abusers. Specifically, the bill makes multi-agency public protection arrangements (MAPPA) between police, prison and probation take account of those convicted (and receiving a sentence of over twelve months) of coercive and controlling behaviour. Sounds good, right? Of course this should happen; most people would wonder why these dangerous violent perpetrators weren't already receiving such monitoring on release from prison, but there you go. We should celebrate that the government is finally doing this.

See what you think – here are my questions to Nicole Jacobs, the Domestic Abuse Commissioner for England and Wales:

Jess Phillips: Nicole, give the Committee an idea of the number of domestic abuse incidents a year.

Nicole Jacobs: Well, according to the Office for National Statistics, it is 2.3 million.

JP: And then those that get reported to the police?

NJ: One in five. Sometimes the research says one in six, but we can say one in five.

JP: One in five of those, so you can all do the maths quickly* – because the Prime Minister tells us that that is important. Last year, the conviction figure on coercive control was 564, so we have gone from 2 million down to 564 that will be affected by this Bill. Of course, it only affects those over 12 months, so I think that is 10% of that 564. Is that correct?

NJ: Yes.

JP: So we are getting down to under 100 victims of domestic abuse actually affected by this Bill. I just want to make sure that I have got that right. Is that correct?

NJ: That is correct for that provision, which is really why I was making the point about the wider work required. Or,

---

* It's 10 million instances of domestic abuse if you can't manage the maths, and if you can't multiply two by five then frankly Rishi Sunak may have had a point about maths being woeful in our country.

as the Bill progresses, I am sure you will have people who might put forward other offences that ought to be included. However, that is correct, and I suppose that not every dangerous perpetrator of domestic abuse will be subject to MAPPA, because of the fact of the lack of convictions.

So around fifty-six extra violent domestic abusers will be monitored in the community. Why bother focusing on the actual problem – the lack of convictions – when you could announce something that sounds really good even if it does only affect fifty-six people in a country of 65 million? I am not against this change; I am against the fact that organisations and people who lobby for these changes are made to feel as if we should genuflect and be grateful for the absolute basics. This should have already been the case! This isn't work on service delivery and tackling this heinous problem, it is righting a proportionally tiny and specific wrong that should never have happened in the first place.

I have given you a couple of really specific illustrations but the examples are, I'm afraid, absolutely legion. Do you feel your area has been levelled up?* If you were to listen to an MP from Stoke-on-Trent in the Commons on the subject of levelling up, you would think that the Potteries

---

* My father has a specific gripe about the term levelling up, in that one cannot level up but instead become level. Even the term speaks to the gamification in politics. Not a big issue, sure, but it annoys him and reminds me of the time my husband horrified a lovely earnest left-wing activist, who had joined me to campaign against Brexit, when he said, 'The worst thing about Brexit is the word Brexit – stupid portmanteau hashtag nonsense.' She tried to plead with him that in fact the worst thing was that thousands of citizens might lose their rights, but he wouldn't be budged.

were now paved with gold. In fact, the Levelling Up Fund built a new car park and a leisure centre that isn't even in Stoke. Hardly brought the area back to its industrial glory years and, shock horror, London still has better transport and more wealth.

There is a reason why saying things like 'Stop the boats' and then not actually doing stuff is allowed to go on, and I'm afraid that very much lies with the overall degradation of our expectations when it comes to what the state, or politics more generally, can actually deliver for us. We have been trained to be grateful for the basics.

Expectations management is a political term most usually bandied around at election times. Basically, political parties have to make out as if they are definitely going to lose loads of seats in the local elections, or that it is going to be incredibly tough in some spurious byelection, so that they can say they were right, no matter the outcome. If they win said byelection or make gains in loads of council seats, then they get to just celebrate. If they don't win, they can declare that they always said it was going to be tough and reach for phrases such as, 'It is always really tricky for government parties in elections midterm, we always knew it was going to be difficult' and, 'Well, we haven't won in this seat for a hundred years so it was always going to be an uphill struggle.' I honestly don't know why the political class do this anymore, it is so painfully transparent as to be an utter embarrassment. Just say, 'I really hope we win because I like winning; losing feels like pain and I'd rather be popular than loathed.'

Before an election there is literally no light shed by any

political party about what the actual outcome will be, because, truth be told, we don't know. We can guess from what we are seeing on the ground; I usually know if I am going to win or not in the weeks leading up to an election, not for certain, but pretty close. If asked in a public forum if I was going to win, I would still probably say, 'It's looking good but we are still fighting for every vote, nothing is in the bag yet.' The answer to the same question off the record would be, 'I bloody hope I win.'

There is often a funny moment in the pre-election expectations management game where you may have managed expectations so well as to have led the voters to believe that you cannot possibly win and so there is little point in bothering to go out and vote for you. At this point you have to show a bit of leg and start briefing that things are looking positive, get a journalist to write a story about how close the election is – we call this 'squeeze messaging'. It's to squeeze out the votes and make people think that the whole election hinges on their single cross in a box. I remember during the Tamworth byelection, where I was posted for four weeks to help campaign, how we went on and on about how we would need a historic level of swing in the vote to win it: we had a nearly 20,000 majority to overturn and this was the kind of result you never get. At the point where it looked like we needed to shift a big chunk of the 'don't know' voters, I was dispatched to speak to all the journalists that I knew (pretty much every single Westminster hack) about how I thought that the Tory vote was collapsing and that, say it quietly, it was looking not certain but a possible win for Labour. We won by 1,316 votes in the end, and it was indeed an historic victory.

We do a lot of expectations management when it comes to elections. As all political parties do this, and any politician worth their salt could do it in their sleep, I wonder why we are so utterly shit at managing expectations in every other regard. One of the main problems with politics today is the woeful mismatch between reality and the expectations of the public.

This problem is two-fold and oddly paradoxical. The public have exceedingly high expectations of what is actually possible and simultaneously appallingly low expectations after years and years of decline. I shall deal with the latter first.

'Can I put extra bin bags out as I've not had a collection for two weeks?' reads the message that I sent to my office WhatsApp group as we entered the new year of 2024. Very festive, I know. I had said Happy New Year already. I am not so useless that I need my staff to collect my dry cleaning for me (who actually does dry cleaning, is it even still a thing?) or to keep me up to date with the refuse collection schedule in our local area. Really specifically, John, who works in my office, used to be the cabinet member on Birmingham City Council in charge of the bins, so I knew he would know the stuff they don't tell you about how you can get away with putting a few extra bags out over Christmas. What then ensued was my staff moaning about their spiralling rubbish mountains and the change in the recycling collection rota. So far so normal. I was instructed that, yes, I could get away with a few extra bags outside my wheelie bin.

On the day of the collection, I had put out my recycling, my normal wheelie bin and three extra black bin bags. I had absolutely zero confidence that all three would be gone but thought, *Sod it, the worst that can happen is I'll have to bring them back in.* I awoke the next morning to the delicious sound of cascading smashing wine bottles being emptied into the bin lorry, which meant my recycling was being taken. I leaped up like a child on Christmas morning: was it possible I could succeed in the triple? Would my bins, my recycling and the extra bags all be taken? I pulled back my bedroom curtains, flooding the room with light, to see that I had only gone and done the bloody hat-trick. Back of the net. I did a little dance as if I had won the bloody lottery.

So low were my expectations of basic public services that I danced a jig to celebrate my bins being collected. The fact that they hadn't been collected over the Christmas period never gave me a moment's pause. Why would I expect that basic public services in the second-largest city in the UK – one of the richest countries in the world – a city where at least a third of the people don't even celebrate Christmas, shouldn't completely cease?

I text my brother who lives in a small town, not a city, in northern France. It is in an ex-mining area – let's call it the Rotherham of France. He tells me that there they have twice-weekly bin collections for household waste, once a week for recycling, and once a week for compost through the summer months.* Can you imagine such a service? My God, I would be giddy; I'm not sure I would be able to cope, the little dances would have to be kept for special occasions.

It is not just successful bin collections that I have learned to fetishise. Recently I could be found in the salons and cafes of south Birmingham raving about how, when I had applied for my youngest son's passport, it had come within the two-week timeframe. When it popped through my letterbox within the allocated time, I actually rang my husband in glee. *Glee!*

I cannot give more examples of low expectations being exceeded because there aren't any. I have for at least two years allocated five hours' travel time to get to work in London from my home in Birmingham each week, a journey that should take two hours door to door, because my expectation is that the train I am booked on – of which there used to be four an hour and now only two – will be cancelled. I've adapted to the disappointment. If I am sick, I leave it the maximum amount of time to try to get a doctor's appointment in the hope that I will get better by myself, because I know that getting a GP appointment will take two weeks not two hours. I rang nineteen dental practices, trying to get an NHS dentist and could find not one possible appointment; the only option was to be a

---

* After I asked this question on the family WhatsApp and explained it was research for my book, my brother Luke cast shade on how riveting it sounded and suggested the title: *Refuse Management in the Pas-de-Calais – Bin Waiting Too Long.*

private patient, in which case I could have had an appointment that day.

These minor erosions in my own expectations for public services are nothing compared to the utterly crushing work I have to do as a constituency MP. Telling a family who are homeless through no fault of their own that they will be on a housing waiting list for a minimum of two years has become so normal that I could just be replaced with a dejected tape recording of my voice that simply says: 'You will be better off looking for a private rental, which I absolutely know that you cannot afford to sustain and are scared of because your current landlord has just turfed you out of your home with no good reason, than finding social housing.' I can't get a dentist's appointment on the NHS, but I am not living with three kids in a single room in unsafe, unclean temporary accommodation next door to someone who just came out of prison for grievous bodily harm after eighteen months, so I'll count my blessings.

When a 22-year-old rape victim sits in front of me and explains how hard it was to tell the police about her uncle abusing her throughout her childhood but she is glad she did it, I almost want to lie to her about what will happen next. I want to say, 'The investigation will take a few weeks and then you should be in court within six months.' I remember headier days when I used to moan about that being too long. Now I have to tell her that it will likely take a year for even a slim possibility of a charge to be brought against her rapist. In that time, it will take over six months to get evidence off his phone, and the forensic evidence she has given over – a pair of knickers or swabs from an invasive examination – will take at least nine months to come back from the lab. (But, sure, police forces across the country are going to manage wholesale drug-testing of everyone!) I have become part of the industry that allows the disappointment to be normalised. I forewarn her that even after a year waiting for a charge to be brought, the likelihood is that she will wait another two years to get the case into a UK courtroom. And all the while said uncle will be free to walk the streets, may well be at family weddings and funerals with her in the intervening years, and, at the end of all that, the likeliest thing is that he will either not be charged (currently 97.8 per cent likely) or be found not guilty even if he is charged (25 per cent likely).

Why are we not taking to the barricades? Years of austerity policies have cut our public services to the bone. For those with enough, this has led to extra costs and some petty annoyances. For those with very little, it will have been in the worst cases the difference between life and death. For me, it has cost me hundreds of hours of productivity, but for the people I meet week in, week out it will have cost them a prosperous future. Your life is damned if you are a victim of crime who gets no justice. Think of the children taken into the care system because their mother couldn't access family support services or children's social services to live free from a domestic abuser. Even if she could have, she would have had to live in a hotel for over a year with her kids, likely many miles from their school and support networks. How well do you think your kids would do in their GCSEs if they had to study for them while living in a hotel room with their entire family at a service station on the M6?

Austerity didn't work: it ramped up trillions in the cost of social ills, but for me the very worst element of it is that we all learned to expect so much less. Not just to expect so much worse, but to receive a crappy service at the same time as being annoyed that any of our taxes were being spent on any services because they simply weren't serving us. We were taught to be grateful for the absolute bare minimum level of service and to be appalled at the spiralling cost of services that were not working. 'Why am I paying my council tax when the libraries are all shutting, the roads are full of potholes and my bin collection was missed again this week? What exactly am I paying the highest rates of tax in seventy years for?'

I've met George Osborne and David Cameron; I do not believe them to be either hardworking or clever enough to have had this as their master plan all along: to utterly undermine people's feelings towards the state to the point where they no longer believe that the state can actually function as a support in their lives; to manufacture a situation where services were so degraded that funding the state itself from taxes at all was called into question by the masses.

Perhaps I should give them more credit; they are two very rich men, from families who would never have struggled financially beyond the possible embarrassment of being found to have had money hidden away in offshore tax havens. They definitely believe that they've got where they are because they are very clever men. Had either of them had to study for their A-levels in a Travelodge at a motorway service station I suspect they would have struggled to make it to Oxford University (although, to be fair, the M40 services are a cut above). Their life and upbringing will not have been one where they believed that the state had a role in their successes, so the likelihood is that their conservatism was such that they wanted to see services degraded, social security diminished and taxes lowered. To do that, you first have to wean people off the idea that they should expect anything from the state, and persuade them that their money would be better spent paying as individuals for services such as education, health, dentistry than going on taxes. Bravo, boys, job done. What a fantastic legacy.

But those who followed Cameron and Osborne really levelled up those low expectations. Less stealthy in its approach, very much an in-your-face phase of degradation.

I feel a bit bad for airbrushing out Theresa May in this because she was simply just so utterly and completely paralysed by Brexit divisions in the country and in Westminster that she can barely be considered to have done anything at all. I always thought that on her gravestone it would read: 'She did a review.' She never actually did anything; even with the passable stuff she wanted to do, she basically just started a consultation on the issue, like paternity leave or stopping sexual harassment at work. Even the Domestic

Abuse Bill, which she set in motion, changed very little and the actual on-the-ground effect is about as groundbreaking as a garden trowel. So, I am afraid, she is to be airbrushed.

It was Boris Johnson who really lowered expectations; not in terms of public services, that work was already well underway by the time he came to power. No, his forte was to make people completely and utterly disillusioned with the institution of politics itself. Give him his dues, at this he was a master. Unless you were asleep for a decade you couldn't have avoided knowing that Boris Johnson was a lying, cheating, nepotistic, party-throwing, sexist, racist, homophobic dilettante. If I had a pound for every time someone said to me in the Johnson years, 'The trouble is, the public have just baked in that he is a liar' then I would be able to pay the child support for any one of the unknown number of his offspring.

Let me pause to express what a charlatan Boris Johnson was, as someone who has met him numerous times and had various conversations with him. He is not a big, bold, funny character. He is a shy and withering man in real life. I have never had a conversation with him where he didn't look utterly terrified of me. His demeanour is the same as that of a teenager caught smoking a fag who goes silent and kicks his feet or picks at a stray thread on his cuff for fear of making eye contact. The heart of a lion does not beat in his chest . . . the heart of a shrew, maybe. He has never, in my presence, said anything remotely funny or charming, never acted with bombast or as a raconteur. There was a period where, no matter what I raised with him in person about issues of domestic abuse or the violent rhetoric he was encouraging about politicians being traitors, he would look uncomfortable and finally resort to merely spluttering, 'We must get Brexit done', like a wind-up doll. He is physically shorter than me because he stoops, and even wearing a slight heel made me feel as if I was towering over him. He is not quick-witted, cannot come up with a snappy retort to gentle ribbing; he wouldn't last a minute working behind a bar and his entire schtick is a marketing ploy. However, to be fair to Boris Johnson, he could at least compute what I was saying, whereas from the brief interactions I have had with the man who Johnson made his chancellor of the exchequer, I suspect he has either never met a person with a Birmingham accent before or is in fact an automaton who had not had the necessary 50p fed into his meter when I came across him. Blank as a sheet of paper is my review on Rishi Sunak.

Anyway, back to the point. Boris Johnson set in train such low expectations about the morality and behaviour of the political class that it became just general wallpaper to assume bad faith in politics. It wasn't even the throwing of illegal parties during lockdown, or overseeing a governance structure that thought nothing of handing out billions of pounds of taxpayers' money, jobs and peerages to friends and lovers, that was the worst degradation. His own loose relationship with the truth, presented as a fake positivity schtick about what was actually possible and was being achieved, set us on a terrible collision course for disappointment and low expectations.

Brexit is the most obvious and egregious example of us being told that there was some sunlit upland of world trade that was going to see UK plc replicating the American gold rush. He was like a teenager who hadn't done his homework. He just kind of assumed it would all be okay. But it very clearly wasn't. He could say whatever he wanted, but the legal and literal reality was very different. It isn't just the overall problems of Brexit clearly contracting the UK's economic growth, but also at each individual part of the process along the way Johnson would make out, like Trump in America, that it was the greatest deal in the world, it was 'oven ready'. Apart from it not being ready at all.

Levelling up similarly was going to redress all the economic disparities between the north and the south, and he would speak about it as if he was Helen of Troy launching a thousand ships on a coastline rather than a car park in Stoke.

Low expectations are a cancer to politics. They allow really bad-faith actors to get away with murder and deliver absolutely nothing. We have all learned to genuflect in gratitude if something works, and just to be fatigued by this week's scandal about another government promise undelivered or fraud in government contracts. There is too much failure for us to hang our hats on each thing and so, like anyone in an abusive relationship, we just learned to accept our fate and be grateful for the days we didn't take a beating.

The trouble is, and here is the paradox, people's

expectations are at the same time phenomenally low and far too high. For some reason, we have lost the art of understanding that things take time; that overhauling systems, changing landscapes and working for improvements is hard and complex. We have been trained to accept that if our house was burgled, it is perfectly normal to wait seven days for a police officer to visit our home and simply give us a crime reference for the incident so we can claim on our insurance, and for there to be no hope of catching the culprits. All while being utterly impatient or truly trying and failing to understand that adapting policing in our country for the modern world will take years and effort on the part of everybody. We just settle on the idea that policing in our country has gone to the dogs and there is nothing to be done. It should be exactly the other way around. Basics should be expected; complexities and long-term change should be tolerated.

I won't start a wholesale criticism of the voter for this. Sloganeering has led us here and that has existed in politics for as long as I have been alive. I don't hate a slogan if it leads to an outcome. 'Education, education, education,' said Tony Blair before reducing class sizes in the UK and rebuilding hundreds of schools. 'From the cradle to the grave,' said the Beveridge Report, which Atlee took into the 1945 general election and led to the creation of the NHS to care for us from birth to death among many other things. 'There is no alternative' was a slogan about capitalism that Thatcher favoured and, to be fair to her, she stuck pretty firmly to delivery against it. Using marketing to promote your ideas and sell them fast to a busy and disinterested electorate is totally understandable, but then you actually have to deliver against it through a process of hard-detailed and often pretty slow transition.

'Take back control' meant nothing and delivered nothing; see also 'Make America Great Again'. I would be fine with 'take back control' if it had led to people in the UK, after a long transition of various different policies outside of the European Union, being given more control over their lives, their workplaces, their choices. If Trump had made America great again by any metric, even just better at one thing than it had been before, I would say it was so. When you boil down really complex things to a few words and act triumphalist when that wins rather than being humbled and ready to do the hard work of change, then the end result is just people feeling really despondent and certain that in fact nothing can change for anything but the worse.

Utter rubbish; loads can change. It is entirely realistic for me to say that, with the required amount of effort, resource, goodwill and time, we could in the next decade build a social care service for the disabled and elderly our country will be as proud of as the NHS. I can say with a completely straight face that in a decade the UK could be almost entirely energy self-sufficient, and that growth in green tech will not just be good for our planet but also for our bills and our overall economy. These exact things have already happened in the past. The unthinkable has become possible: the NHS was created, the Industrial Revolution made our country rich, women got the vote. Along the way we have eliminated loads of ills in society, like diseases that kill millions, massively reduced* teen pregnancies, invented the internet . . . you know, just small things. Stuff does and can change; we have just got to stop expecting it to be as easy as a three-word slogan. Saying 'Stop the boats' over and over again is not the same as sorting our massively clogged-up immigration system, trying to genuinely stop the trade in people across the Channel with some actual law enforcement, or working with leaders from across the world on the issue of mass migration which is not going anywhere, unless we can hurry up and stop the rain from falling instead. None of this is easy, it is hard, and mistakes will be made along the way, but we should at the very least have higher expectations than we currently do to believe it is possible.

We need to go to the barricades to fight for the basics to be better and chuck out our lowly expectations at the same time as having big, bold expectations for the future. If we don't do this, we are going to continue to expect our politicians to lie to us, constantly announcing things that sound like a sea change but at best will be a dribble. I don't want you to tell me you have a policy about drug-testing every person who enters a police station unless you can actually do it, and doing it has an actual outcome like

---

* Between 2007 and 2021, the under-eighteen conception rate in England and Wales decreased by 68 per cent, thanks to changes made to education and the availability of contraception. I can think of three girls when I was at school who left to have a baby; my sons by comparison don't know a single girl in their school who faced the same situation.

reduced crime and drug deaths. The soundbite not backed up by action must end. Only deeds will do. Let's demand deeds.

5

Courage Calls to Courage Everywhere

When I was elected to parliament I had been inside the building maybe two or three times before. My husband had only been to London once before. While I had been deeply involved in politics all my life it mostly concerned local Labour Party campaigning, or local renewal schemes in my neighbourhood. Where my political education was national in scope, it was issue-based. I had been in and out of the Home Office and the Ministry of Justice, advising on legislation regarding gang violence and modern slavery, for example. The home secretary or justice secretary of the day would come out to do photo opportunities in my places of work, women's refuges or youth violence projects. I kid you not, when David Cameron was prime minister he and Eric Pickles came to a youth offending and gang violence project I was working on and we were given thousands of pounds of funding (which we could have done with to actually help youth offenders) to put in a graffiti installation for the visit, you know, to help Dave look a bit urban. I believe he was hugging hoodies at the time. The fact that graffiti art is largely done by people in their forties and has next to no hinterland in youth culture (seriously, if you were to commission a graffiti artist today to do a piece, I bet they'd be forty-five and vegan) was of no interest to those taking the photo. I have never once worked with a young person who has been criminally exploited into a county lines gang or into sexual or drug-based slavery who has ever picked up a can of spray paint in their lives.

Anyway, I digress – what I am saying is that my politics is personal. It is driven by the people I have met and worked with. People who have fuck all and would think someone utterly mad to spend a thousand quid on making a bloke who drinks his pints in the Cotswolds look a bit edgy. My politics comes from exposure to the worst of people's lives, communities ravaged by arson attacks, so scared of their neighbours that they turn on each other. Children growing up in care who are left at the mercy of organised crime. Women brutally abused so many times that you have to arrange for the third time working with them for children's services to come and remove the new baby they are pregnant with. I once had to hold the neck of a woman who had slashed it in front of me while I was sat at my desk, desperately trying to stem the flow. I have held the hands of children while they waved off their sibling who had been adopted while they were not. I have seen things, heard stories and intervened in the kind of dangerous environments that would make the toughest, burliest men cry. I have, in fact, since becoming an MP been the only person in a group otherwise consisting of men to take charge when someone was suffering an angry psychotic episode. When I was recently asked to take part in a TV fly-on-the-wall programme inside a prison, I concluded that I would not make good telly as I have worked in prisons and would be largely unflappable, and would most likely within minutes be able to get the inmates on my side.

I am currently owed two amounts of compensation, which will never come, from violent men who I put myself in front of in order to protect the woman they were attacking. When those women felt that they couldn't go through with the process of bringing charges, I did instead. Fancy being so unlucky that you decided to headbutt your girlfriend in broad daylight on a street in Tamworth when I was driving down the road having been out campaigning in the byelection. Not to put too fine a point on it, by most people's standards I am nails.

I have always been tough. I grew up with three brothers all older than me and feminist parents who never for a second allowed me to think toughness or conflict were the preserve of men. Add to that the years and years of working in institutions where instantaneous risk assessments have taught me to intervene safely in a dangerous situation. Mix all that up with the privilege of knowing you will get a better police response because of your position and what you get is someone with the courage and knowledge to stop a fight. On the night of the 2019 general election, I had a camera crew from a documentary production company following me around. I was driving home at 11 p.m. from my office, where I had been campaigning for a solid fifteen hours, with the crew all cramped in the back of my car with their sound and filming equipment. I was heading home to change before I was due at the election count in Birmingham City centre that evening to find out if I had won. It was by no means a done deal and there was a very real chance I was about to lose my job. On the drive home from my office, I saw a woman struggling to get away from a man. So I stopped my car and approached them. No one else in my car joined me. They sat in the back, terrified by the situation. I managed to get the woman into my car and told the man that if he didn't leave her alone, I was calling the police who would, because it was me, come quick smart. I copped an earful from him but, whatever, mate, I've heard worse – after all, I've been trying to get people to vote all day. My tolerance level for people annoyed at my presence is pretty high. After some negotiations with the woman, we settled that I would take her to her mother's and from there she would call the police if she felt she wanted to. I knew and she knew that this would likely lead to no action, even though I had been witness to her perpetrator's behaviour, but she told me she would. So off we went, me expected at my own election count ceremony, to take a woman to a place of safety. I called my mate Alex, who was due to join me at the count, and asked her to stay with the woman for a while because I was anxious I might miss my declaration. I am not sure there are many Members of Parliament who would do this.

I don't say this to blow my own trumpet ... well, not entirely. I say it because I think it speaks to the kind of politician I am. The roll-up-your-sleeves, get-your-hands-dirty, get-dug-in kind of person. I was a senior manager at the organisation where I worked before I was an MP. I was called on to advise secretaries of state but that didn't mean I wasn't also co-opted to build bunk beds for arriving families, butter baps for celebration buffets or sew curtains long after my shift had finished because the previous tenant had set fire to the last pair.

I had no expectations of parliament when I was elected, I really had no idea what I was entering into, but I assumed that anyone who was frankly mad enough to get themselves elected would be brave if nothing else. It is a fundamentally brave thing to do: to put yourself up for intense levels of personal scrutiny and vitriol for the sake of ideals you hold is, I think, the very definition of courage. Yes, it more than doubled my salary when I was elected so for me it was a smart career move as well, but fundamentally it is an incredibly tough gig in personal terms for that professional boost. I have written extensively before about this: whether you like them or not, 90 per cent of MPs take on the job because they are driven by the desire to improve things, either generally or specifically.

Yes, I think elected office is noble and only something the brave can do. This, of course, before you factor in what is now a quite dangerous environment of hatred and violence aimed at politicians. If police officers or social workers were murdered at the relative rate that MPs have been in the last decade, hundreds of them would be dead. I was elected in 2015 and two of those elected that day, out of a total of 650, have been murdered, another only narrowly avoiding a genuine plot to behead her. The only police officer, for comparison, who was murdered in this time period was Keith Palmer, who was killed by a terrorist in parliament seeking to kill MPs. There are 170,000 police officers and only 650 MPs. Our murder rate is pretty high. I literally cannot remember how many cases I have taken to court because of the threat to me, but two men have served years in prison for threatening to rape and/or kill me. One remains in my local prison today. So, yes, I think it is brave to be an MP.

It is for this reason that one of the things that I noticed about parliamentary politics when I was elected, something that I truly hadn't expected, was how this courage evaporates in the face of political party machines and the pursuit of power.

It is not that individuals are not personally courageous, most are. I say most – about half would absolutely stick their necks out for a cause that wasn't universally popular. Almost all are courageous in the face of injustices that have befallen their constituents; what is less common is those who are courageous in the face of their own political party or when in opposition to their constituents.

Make no mistake, I am only an MP by virtue of the Labour Party. Not only do I rely on the institution for all of the backroom administrative support, namely the data systems that all political parties depend on, but I also rely on them for pretty much 95 per cent of my votes. While I assume that you are keen on me as a politician because you have bothered to pick up a book I have written, and I like to think that my constituents are pretty pleased with the service that I offer to them as their MP, the truth is that people voting for me are actually voting for the Labour Party. Only the truly arrogant would think that they could win as an independent and have anything more than one term in politics. See George Galloway for your best example.

Political parties matter, despite how much we choose to rail against two-party systems around the world. The debt I owe to the Labour Party, over my lifetime and the lifetime of my parents and grandparents, is immense. However, I also literally owe them my job and they can take it away should I displease them. With the single stroke of a pen the Labour Party could, in the national executive committee meeting, no longer support my candidacy as a Labour MP and it's sayonara, Jess Phillips MP. It is right, then, that I have to keep the Labour Party onside. The question I always ask myself in the times when I have had to speak up against this institution I both love and respect, but also am to all intents and purposes employed by, is: do I stay quiet for the sake of my job, the sake of the party, or the sake of the country/cause?

This is the order in which I prioritise:

1. Country
2. Constituents

3. Party

4. Me

I am a party loyalist and sometimes doing what is best to keep the party on track is, in the long run, better for the country. The root of this conviction lies in the fact that personally (let's face it, factually) I believe the country (in that I mean the vast majority of its inhabitants) is always better off under a Labour government. I wouldn't live away from my family and my superior Birmingham-based pillows for half of my life if I didn't. However, sometimes this is a cop-out, and also a tactic of control used by political parties to keep their loyal flock in order. 'If you speak out on this you will damage the party and that is only good for the other side.' Sometimes this is true; sometimes it roughly translates to, 'Shut up about your thing, we don't want to deal with it.'

I must say that if you moan about absolutely everything in your political party and you create special named gangs like the European Research Group, or Popular Conservatism, then you are still usually thinking about yourself and most likely you are complaining in order to cause trouble within your own ranks because you're rolling the pitch for someone else to be the leader of your party. Usually, people sign up to these groupings who are just trying to cause trouble because they think it would be better for them if this week's show-off were to be in charge. Insert Boris Johnson or Liz Truss here. People cannot truly be striving for what either of these two represented or achieved because it was,

respectively, absolutely nothing and absolute fucking calamity. The priorities of the members of the parliamentary
Conservative Party, with everyone seemingly joining some
inanely entitled gang, were as follows:

1. Themselves (they literally think they will get a better
    job under the next fool)
2. Constituency (note I didn't write constituents; I wrote
    constituency because it isn't the people who live there
    that they care about, they are just worried about losing
    their seat)
3. The media. Mark Francois, for example, loves to moan
    at his political party. He, an absolute nobody, literally
    commanded the entire political lobby to a press con-
    ference he was holding to speak for what he actually
    dubbed, with a straight face, the 'five families' groups
    in the Conservative Party. Everyone in Westminster
    knows Francois is at best a pillock, at worst, well,
    much worse, and yet his little moment of dissent
    (moaning at the PM) meant he got some attention and
    thought while the lights shone on him he would liken
    himself to Don Corleone from *The Godfather*, who, by
    the way, I would sooner share a taxi with.
4. That's it, there isn't a fourth.

Do not mistake this type of self-promotion for bravery to
speak out against the party. It is completely selfish, but it
fills column inches so on it goes. When I resigned from
the Labour Party frontbench in 2023, I did not do it easily.

I did not call a press conference of the nation's media out onto the green outside parliament to hear my woes; I did not liken myself to anyone from *The Godfather*, mainly because the women in it are usually abused by the men or (spoiler alert) shot dead after a memorably bad performance.* Instead, I did everything I possibly could in private to get to a workable solution within my party.

I resigned from the frontbench position I held in the Labour opposition in order to vote for an immediate ceasefire in hostilities in Israel and Gaza. I have written before about how the hardest thing that we have to do as politicians is vote on military action and war. People wrongly think that no war is always the best solution, and so politicians come under enormous scrutiny when voting on bomb-dropping and boots on the ground in far-flung places. Of course, in an ideal world no war is the best solution – congratulate yourself for reaching the analytical level on geopolitics of a Miss World contestant. Sometimes military action is required; if we could all have our time again, I am fairly certain the body politic both here and in the US would try to use military power in order to stop Bashar al-Assad from gassing those people in Syria that he didn't displace. The mass global migration that sees children's bodies bobbing lifeless in the English Channel can be directly linked back to our desire not to intervene in foreign conflicts. Hotel rooms in my constituency are filled with Syrian families and Eritrean men fleeing unpaid

---

* Seriously, skip *The Godfather Part III*.

conscription to the army, which they would face if they stayed at home. Don't think ever that doing nothing means no one dies; people die no matter what. Sometimes the bravest thing to do against immense pressure is to vote to engage UK forces in war.

The Israel/Gaza situation was slightly different because the UK's armed forces were not engaged in the fighting, precluding the need for a decision on possible deployment from our politicians. The only role, if at all, that the UK had in this conflict when it started was as an ally of Israel, and in theory we have some influence with Israeli officials. I say in theory because in actual fact it is only the US that has any real influence with Israel, but as the closest ally of the US in the world we can influence them, as can France, Germany, etc. The UK government and parliament had an opportunity as an ally to set a tone on how we expected the war to progress; we could establish parameters of tolerance, show what would and would not have our support. We could also seek other forms of leverage such as financial sanctions on those we consider to be the aggressor, as was done when Russia invaded Ukraine. It may not work, it wouldn't have in Syria and it made not a jot of difference in Ukraine, but failing all else it is the only influence we have in conflicts we are not directly engaged in.

The massacre that Israel suffered on 7 October 2023 was the worst attack on Jewish people since the Holocaust. Brutal acts of killing, raping and hostage-taking by the terrorists from Hamas shocked the world. There should be no doubt in anyone's mind (other than conspiracy cranks) that Israel had no choice but to respond with force in order to crush a terrorist group that threatened the safety and lives of its people and seek to get back the hundreds of hostages taken in the attack. If a member of my family were taken hostage by a neighbouring terror group it is what I would expect of the UK government. In fact, there were UK nationals taken hostage on that day and, what seemed inexplicable, many Thai people who were working in Israel at the time. It was absolutely right under these circumstances that the UK government supported Israel in their endeavours to free our citizens and to quell the threat posed by Hamas, who helpfully took to the airwaves to say they would do it all again.

As the massacre unfolded, I was, along with almost all my colleagues, at the Labour Party conference. The Labour Party has a long history of support for the recognition of the Palestinian state. This is a position I hold firmly and, if truth be told, judging by the visits I have made to the occupied territories, no one could leave there thinking that the Israeli government led by Benjamin Netanyahu was anything but brutal and oppressive towards the Palestinian population. I wholeheartedly support the Palestinian people and their need for statehood; however, in the face of such a brutal massacre it was without doubt a time to show complete solidarity with the Israeli people. I made sure that I went to find people at the event – journalists, parliamentary candidates, Members of Parliament and of the House of Lords – who were Jewish and had family in Israel and showed them solidarity and love. I remember a conversation with one lovely colleague about how it would ignite a tinderbox in the region and how, at a moment when good political leadership was required, Netanyahu was not the person they wanted in charge at this time because he would worsen not improve the situation. Never has a more obvious analysis been made.

Worsen it did, and the offensive undertaken by Israel saw none of the world-leading targeting intelligence we are constantly told it has and instead has resulted in the complete and utter destruction of Gaza. If you are one of the lucky ones not to be among the thousands of people who have been killed in Gaza, you have been internally displaced and every bit of infrastructure – hospitals, schools, roads, homes – has been destroyed. Palestinian people in Gaza are as much victims of Hamas as anyone else, and yet their lives are being wiped out one way or another by the action taken by Netanyahu against the terror group. If they are not being bombed they are being starved by the restrictions on getting aid into Gaza, which is entirely in the gift of Netanyahu.

While this situation was worsening towards the end of 2023, it appeared that in the UK parliament we were simply signalling that Israel had our full support. Yes, our leaders were saying that Israel must act with restraint, but when they didn't we continued to say it: 'Israel has our full support' – well, it didn't have mine. There is no situation I can think of where I would give Benjamin Netanyahu, a man hated by most Israelis and by no means voted for by the majority of them thanks to a proportional representation system of election (all those who hail it as the best solution for democracy take note), my full support in anything. He is, in my opinion, a massive racist and awaiting trial for many charges of corruption, so also likely a crook. Yes, before the events of 2023 some argued the benefits of maybe keeping him onside to a degree so that we could try to influence him, but to constantly assert that he had our full support was in my mind a mistake. Mistake is perhaps too small a word for signalling support for the indiscriminate killing of masses of people. People who, I have absolutely no doubt in saying, Netanyahu believes simply don't matter as much as his people. He considers them lesser. How can I give that my support?

The simple matter is that I supported the calls for a ceasefire in Gaza. I thought, as turned out to be the case, that a negotiated ceasefire would be the best way to achieve the release of hostages taken by Hamas. Some had themselves been accidentally shot and killed by the Israel Defense Forces, and some will have died in the bombardment by Israel. Many more were released when a ceasefire, albeit temporary, was negotiated. I am not some peacenik hellbent on no action, but I could not, in the only environment where we as politicians could exert influence in this battle, not try to set a tone.

I had to choose to act against the wishes of my political party. I want to state this as clearly as I possibly can, many of those who did not vote the same way as me did it for entirely noble reasons. Not voting for the ceasefire does not mean they didn't want one; every single person, even the most hawkish MPs, wanted a ceasefire. Many will have made the decision based on the fact that voting for it would make no difference at all unless the motion was passed, which it wouldn't be because the Conservative majority would not vote for it. It may have made not a jot of difference even if it had passed, because the PM can say and do whatever they want regardless of parliament's view – long gone is the old-fashioned consensus of the executive listening to the concerns of the elected representatives. Many will have decided that staying on the inside and pushing would be better. Don't get me wrong, others will have just been keeping their heads down, deciding it was not an issue that was worth the fight.

I held a position in the Labour Party as the Shadow Minister for Domestic Abuse and Safeguarding. Had I held this job in government, it would have been the realisation of my life's work in this field. I don't want to blow my own trumpet but there is literally no one elected in the UK and much of the world who would be better suited for this job than me. I am an actual expert in this area, and, what is more, I have the faith of the organisations who work in this sector and, more importantly, I have the trust of the victims. This is rare. My taking up this role in government would not just have been a plaudit for me, it would have represented something to those people – hope for change in our country. To walk away from this chance was not something I could take lightly.

There wasn't really a choice for a number of reasons. First, my principles: I simply couldn't personally stomach being asked to abstain on something I truly believed in. Yes, it might not make the blindest bit of difference but if I spent my political career only speaking up for stuff that would definitely end in the outcome I desired, I would have been completely silent for the past twenty years. I want to see the end of all domestic abuse and sexual abuse against adults and children, an outcome I will literally never live to see, nor will my children, which doesn't mean I shouldn't speak up for it every single day. I have for nine years been campaigning to change the laws on sexual harassment in the workplace, have held rally days, garnered signatures, taken part in reviews and inquiries, made recommendations, moved amendments, begged! Still nothing has changed. Should I stop saying it because it won't happen? I ostensibly spend much of my political life fighting for Hail Marys. I try not to speak on issues I know nothing about* or that do not affect my constituents. By the way, I represent plenty of British Palestinians from Gaza.

It would be an absolute lie for me to assert that, even though my principles were truly aligned with my constituents', the weight of feeling from my people on the matter didn't play a major role in my decision. It did. Not, as has been suggested by many, because of aggression from people in my constituency. I literally suffered not even one single moment of that. People often say that it's aggressive when

---

* I once had to cover for a colleague from the frontbench in a debate in the Commons about seasonal workers' visas and the effect on daffodil farming in Devon and Cornwall. I think this is the only time in my life where I read out a speech written for me by someone else.

it is a largely non-white cohort pushing for something. Yes, I represent a large Muslim population; among them is a tiny minority of cranks and idiots, just like every other demographic I represent. There are anti-vaxxers, antisemites, Islamophobes, plain old-fashioned sexists and racists – we, like everywhere else, have got them all. Yes, people were upset by what they saw as all political parties giving a blank cheque to the military actions in Gaza; some were impassioned, none were aggressive. No one told me I had to vote one way or another or else. Mostly, the way it was represented to me was as pleading, desperation and sadness. One bloke designed a leaflet he was going to de-liver in his neighbourhood that included photos and quotes from Israeli government officials, such as: 'There will be no electricity, no food, no fuel, everything is closed. We are fighting animal people and we are acting accordingly' (Defence Minister Yoav Gallant). His leaflet was asserting that British politicians were in support of this. Could seem pretty aggressive, I suppose, but here's the thing: before he was going to distribute it, he popped into my office, sadly while I was out in Westminster, to leave me a copy to look over. I didn't know this man, but his number was on the leaflet. So I called him up and asked him to come in and have a chat with me. He agreed immediately and said he wouldn't put anything out until we had spoken. He was in no way a crank or aggressive; he was just a man who was devastated by what he saw happening to people in Palestine and was going to use the only tool he had at his disposal – political campaigning, to try to push his local representatives. I have literally spent my career encouraging people to take this kind of action to change things. He was reassured by my words and no leaflet was distributed. In effect his campaigning worked – he expressed his firmly held views to me. Incidentally, he has since dropped in treats for my staff, bought us plants for the office to brighten it up and frequently sends me messages saying he hopes I'm eating and sleeping well as he worries about the stress my job causes me. What a brute!

Yes, people felt strongly about this issue and they told me about it. Did I worry that if I didn't vote for a ceasefire, I would lose the support of these people and then possibly also my seat? Of course I did. If truth be told, there was no choice about resigning from my position on the frontbench because there was a fifty-fifty chance I would have lost it anyway. I am not for a second trying to claim that fear about my livelihood didn't come into my decision at all – it did. Had I not agreed with my constituents, however, I am pretty sure I would have voted a different way. I didn't agree with them about Brexit and at no point did I hide that fact, either in how I voted or what I said. So, I feel confident that it wasn't the only factor, but I'd be pretty irresponsible if I didn't take the livelihood of my entire family into consideration. Funnily enough, in the week preceding the vote, when I was racked with indecision about what was the best thing to do, I asked my husband and he said dryly, 'You'll always be able to get another job, and we will be all right no matter what, so don't let that be the decider.' It would seem that for him, too, country, constituency and party come ahead of self, and, bearing in mind he would rather stick pins in his eyes than join a political party, that is pretty good of him.

I had to make a decision to rebel against my party on a matter of principle and to vote with my constituents. 'So what?' you may say. 'If it's the right thing to do and it will make you popular with your people, then it's a no-brainer, right?' Wrong. I really didn't want to rebel; I really didn't want to leave a job I loved and was good at, working alongside brilliant, passionate people. I didn't want the cause that I care so deeply about to lose its momentum. The Labour Party has pledged to halve the incidence of violence against women and girls in a decade; this is a massive undertaking, and it will not happen unless it is driven fiercely from the centre to achieve that goal. I needed to be in that centre, I needed to be a trusted critical friend to the Labour Party from within. This was the hardest part and I had to conclude that I had built up enough influence in this space that I would still be able to continue this work effectively. Time will tell if that was the right call. I have indeed continued the work; I was doing it long before Keir Starmer empowered me to, and I'll still be doing it as I take my last breaths. At the time of writing I am unsure if this gamble will pay off; I am less sure it will than when I took it. I guess if you piss off your political party, they remember. Funnily enough, the people who were kindest to me throughout this process were the whips (who are meant to be the hardnoses) and Keir Starmer himself.

People, including me, often refer to Keir Starmer as my

boss, but he isn't my boss in any traditional sense of the role. He does not in any way interfere in the work that I do either on issues or in my constituency. Really, the model is flawed because the only time a political leader ever has to act like a real-world boss is when you have done something wrong. If I were, for example, to take to Twitter in an out-of-character racist rant, then it would suddenly be very clear who my boss was. But he didn't come down heavy on me. Instead, when I was sat across from him, explaining my decision to quit my job and vote with my head and heart, he showed me kindness and frankly despair at the difficult situation. He encouraged me to stay and listened to my concerns. The decision had been made by this point, though; there was no going back for me.

The other major consideration in coming to the decision to resign was how this would affect the Labour Party. It would be incredibly easy to make a matter of firmly held conscience seem like a party of people fighting like rats in a sack. I could not and would not risk anyone using my decision to aid the Tories. This would be utterly selfish and in the vein of the Tory shenanigans I loathe. I knew that I would be the main story of the rebellion because, while I was not the only person to resign, I was the most famous. I would set the tone publicly and I knew I had to try to get across the complex nuances of politics, something so very often missing.

As luck would have it, I resigned in the same week that Suella Braverman, the then home secretary, was fired for essentially inciting aggression on the streets of London. In her public statement after she was sacked, she pretty much poured poison and petrol (let's face it, she only has these two items in stock) all over Rishi Sunak. She basically left her post screaming, 'I am better than you and you will rue the day you crossed me, Sunak.' I paraphrase, of course. Basically, if I'd said anything that week that was anything less than threatening to leave a horse's head in Starmer's bed, I was by comparison going to look reasonable. Cheers, Suella, literally the only good thing you ever did.

I tried to explain that no great calamity had occurred. It wasn't necessarily how I felt. I felt sad and worried about my decision. I was scared and a bit isolated from my friends in parliament, none of whom had made the same decision. I was worried that I would be pitted against them as some kind of hero and would be isolated further from them. Also, one person so very dear to me who had not, for a legion of reasons, been able to make the same decision as me and consequently faced considerable risk, must be protected at all costs. Holly Lynch, the MP for Halifax to whom this book is dedicated, is the bravest, most principled politician I know. She looks like a small bespectacled teenager, so much so that on more than one occasion when she and I have been together at events people have assumed she is my intern, and in one insulting moment for me at the Westminster Christmas fair a woman selling Christmas puddings asked if she was my daughter. Holly is six years younger than me. Clearly my decision never to moisturise my skin has not paid dividends. People frequently underestimate how tough and clever she is because of how she looks. Holly is hugely well respected, for example, by pretty much every police force and security agency in our country, and I have watched her pull actual secret agents into line with her when she was the shadow security minister. When the history of how the war in Gaza was handled in Westminster is written she will likely go unnoticed by most, but no one in the building was fighting harder for the Palestinian people than Holly. I wish they knew quite what a fierce advocate they have in her.

There could be no risk of the story becoming about Labour splits rather than Palestinian and Israeli lives – for the sake of the people here in the UK who were in need of a Labour government and those in the Middle East who deserved the focus. I remember on my last visit to the occupied territories we were placed with a Palestinian woman who was working for the charity Medical Aid for Palestinians. She was an aid worker who accompanied us to hospitals and medical facilities and gave us briefings on the situation in the West Bank and Gaza. She was in my memory one of the most phenomenally beautiful women I had ever met. At the end of the trip we went out for an evening of revelry in Ramallah. In your head, the occupied Palestinian territories are a dusty, blockaded wreck, I imagine. This is all we see of it on news broadcasts about settler violence or atrocities in Gaza. You have likely become used over the decades to images of people crying over some tragedy. This is no doubt the case now; however, you should know that before this it was also just a place, with bars and restaurants and people going on nights out. In Ramallah we went to a shisha–cum–pizza restaurant and some of our number were so drunk that we somehow managed to get an entire bar of people singing songs. Our guide from Medical Aid for Palestine joined us and, as she was saying goodbye to me after three days together, she started to sob. She told me that she was rarely treated as a human being; usually, people she spoke to made the conflict about themselves and their righteousness. I committed in that moment never to fall into that trap. Here is a test that I learned while working at Women's Aid: always ask yourself if your motivation is whether you can sleep soundly at night or those you profess to care for can. So often the former is the case; being right is not the same as doing right.

Making my decision all about my righteousness, rather than expressing the complexities of the situation, would have failed my self-imposed test. It would have done nothing to help the Palestinian people, and could have harmed the people I represent.

Bravery in politics isn't always about getting a crescendo moment as if you are Hugh Grant slagging off the US president at the climax of the film *Love Actually*, although in a world of clipped-up videos on Twitter this has become the format for adoration. To me, bravery is challenging perceived wisdom and speaking out against your own side's failings as much as the failings of your opponents. I have watched while colleagues and friends have managed to convince themselves that their silence on events is noble. It so often comes back to the idea that showing any kind of dissent is self-harm for your party. I remember, on one of the now many occasions that the Conservative government breached international laws, asking some pretty decent ministers who are well-respected barristers how on earth they could possibly stomach staying in their positions while laws were being broken. Would this not only jeopardise their morals and, frankly, registration as legal professionals, but also would they not then struggle to go back to practising criminal law? If I, for example, was ever against the former justice secretary, Alex Chalk, in a criminal case, I would just say that the defendant was only breaking the law in a 'limited and specific way'. In 2020 the Northern Ireland secretary, Brandon Lewis, said legislation for Britain's internal market would break international law in a 'specific and limited way'. So that's all right, then. I am not sure what laws are not broken in a specific way – burglary isn't breaking the law vaguely.

The excuse a number of them gave me for staying put in a party of international lawbreakers was: 'If I leave, they will just put some other headbanger in my place and then progress on x, y, z will be lost.' The first thing I would say to this excuse is that if your leadership on a specific policy is so poor that it cannot survive without you then you've not done a very good job. Also, it is just utter horseshit and the honest answer is: 'I want to keep my job, not just now but in the future because if you are seen as a troublemaker, no matter how noble, you will always be considered to be a risk.' Don't wade out, by all means, but don't pretend it is for the sake of nobility.

You can think that you have a better chance of changing

things from within, and you can also conclude that your speaking up on an issue might not make the blindest bit of difference, and you can be right on both fronts, but that should be the truth that is told. Also, if you lean on truth-speaking from within you'd better show some results for that in the subsequent years. After giving me this excuse for why they stayed, both these ministers were promoted from lower ministerial office to become secretaries of state in a government that also broke international law a number of times and, under their watch, was trying to make the UK courts deem Rwanda a safe country for refugees regardless of whether or not the evidence supported this. So, give me a fucking break that you were changing it from within. Also, they incidentally made not a jot of progress on the policies that they leaned on as their missions.

What you, the reader, have to decide is this: do you really want bravery in politics? There is absolutely no way governance could actually happen without some iota of collective responsibility enforced by political parties. Without it we would be in ... well, a mess, while the governing party just fight all day and don't worry their little heads with the service delivery they have been tasked with. Sound familiar? I am not asking for open rebellion or a system of political party referenda on every policy it pursues. I am asking people to pick their battles, to have red lines that cannot be crossed and to enforce these for the sake of trust in politics.

The challenge for the average voter to answer is whether you really want the bravery and honesty from politicians you profess to crave. Sorry is the hardest word in politics. It is so rarely uttered even in the face of absolutely monstrous behaviour. If you are found by two separate independent bodies to have sexually harassed your staff, the usual response is to wildly discredit the process, profess your innocence against all the evidence, say you are mentally affected by the accusation and call the complainant a liar. Sorry was what you should have said.

I have been called on to discipline a number of people who I managed over my years as an adult in the workplace. I have sacked people for gross misconduct – this is literally the hardest thing I have had to do in my career, which is saying something. On two occasions I can remember that the decision not to sack someone was made entirely on the basis of their active and sincere remorse for the error they had made. I believed completely in those moments that these people would never make the same mistake again and that they deserved a second chance. Sorrow is incredibly powerful when it is real.

I think that that the country would be very forgiving in the face of genuine remorse. Had Boris Johnson, for example, just been wholeheartedly believably sorry for the lockdown parties in Westminster I think he would have lasted longer. If he hadn't lied to cover it up and shown that his motivation was to save himself rather than be honest to a country in mourning, he might just have got away with it. The public are a surprisingly forgiving bunch if they believe you. However, I am not so sure that you, the voters, would be quite so forgiving of, or open to, sorrow that was about failed policies rather than personal misdemeanours.

Personally, I long for the day when a politician appears on the television in a long-form interview, rather than a two-second gotcha clip, and explains that they are about to start a policy and there are definitely risks attached to it; it may take a long time to bear fruit, and it might not work, but it is absolutely worth giving it a go. In this nirvana I am imagining it would also be possible for things to be stopped if they clearly weren't working without the entire world's media shouting U-turn and flip-flop and someone having to resign or be reshuffled into a nosebleed job. I want to be able to speak realistically rather than hyperbolically about the plans I wish to see put in place. I want to be held accountable for the money spent, the problems that should, if they could, have been foreseen, and I want to tell the truth about what is possible instead of being forced to overstate effects in some hideous beauty pageant.

I think the country is sick of being told that everything is world-beating, or that we are the best in the world. I think ordinary people are perfectly capable of understanding complexities – have you seen their lives, finances, family logistics? They understand compromise. This is never what we deliver to them. Column inch after column inch says Keir Starmer is boring or changes his mind. Even if those things were true, so fucking what? Do you not change your mind when situations shift? Do you want someone who is going to spit in your face and then tell you it is raining, world-beating rain at that?* I am more of a bombastic attention-seeking sort but I wouldn't want everyone to be like me, it would be chaos.

It would take real courage in politics to move to this approach, to start expressing real sorrow when things didn't work. I was actually quite pleased when Rishi Sunak admitted that he hadn't met his pledge on bringing NHS waiting lists down, until he blamed it entirely on striking doctors and nurses and took no responsibility for the years of degradation. Being really sorry means taking personal responsibility and politicians always say, before something happens, 'The buck stops with me'; they think it sounds tough and decisive, then when something does go wrong, it turns out the buck very much stops literally anywhere else. Would you have tolerated Rishi Sunak telling the truth? Would you have liked him to say: 'I never should have made that pledge, it was actually unrealistic and in hindsight I realise that unless I look at all the reasons why people are getting sick, rather than just at a number I am tracking for my own benefit, I won't be able to achieve it. That is going to take much more time than I thought and I am sorry'?

Some of the lack of courage in Westminster that isn't driven by political parties' desire to control their ranks in the pursuit of power – sometimes noble, sometimes not – is because they think that you won't tolerate the truth. The voters have the power to change this, not with crosses in

---

* To be fair, I do think the UK may have world-beating rain, certainly Manchester and Glasgow do.

boxes necessarily, but with how we go about interacting with politics ourselves. If you want courage and truth, you have to not react with vitriol when it is presented to you, regardless of whether it is from the team you most support or not. Seek out long-form analysis (slightly stupid assertion to make to you, who are literally reading a book about politics, bravo you); before you react with emotion, have a think about what you would have done differently, how you might have dealt with the situation. How would you bring down waiting lists? Do you think it is easy? If you do, then you have fallen into the same trap as Rishi Sunak – you, like he did, would fail.

Courage will never be the best currency in politics until it is demanded by the people, and at present too many are happy with flag-waving and being lied to. What you will get then is lies and a flag waved in your face. I enjoy being aggrieved by my opponents as much as the next person – who doesn't love a good old shout at the telly? – but if we just desire grievance, grievance is all we are going to get.

6

Nothing Ever Changes

'Nothing ever changes, you're all the same.' This is one of the most common things I hear when talking to people on their doorsteps. It doesn't quite beat people complaining about the pavements, the tree outside their house, their bins, or the state of the potholes on their road – people really do care about the things they can see immediately out of their front window – but 'nothing ever changes' is a close second.

It is provably untrue that nothing ever changes. Things have changed dramatically in my lifetime alone. When I had my first baby, for example, I was entitled to only six months of maternity allowance benefits; by the time I had my second, the standards had improved, and I was entitled to nine months of support and a year off work. A small thing, granted, but it had literally changed in the three intervening years.

When my parents and in-laws were kids, children could leave school at fourteen and that is exactly what my mother and father-in-law did. My mother was a civil servant as a young adult in the 1960s; she was at the tail end of the era when women who got married had to immediately quit their jobs. Married women were not allowed to work at the civil service. Unimaginable today. When I was, in the early 2000s, going through the recruitment process to become a civil servant in the Home Office, I was told that the tests couldn't be rearranged for me when I asked for a postponement because I needed to go for an ultrasound scan while pregnant with my first child. Similarly, when I was applying to study a master's in social work after my first son had been born, I was told by the student finance department that because I was under the age of twenty-five my access to a loan would be assessed on the basis of my parents' income. When I protested that I hadn't lived with my parents for seven years and hadn't been in any way reliant on them for four years, and that I had my own dependent child, I was told it didn't matter because I wasn't married. Had I been married, I would have been judged on my own household income. I either belonged to my parents or my husband. These things would never happen now.

'Nothing ever changes' is a moan that is often accompanied by the refrain that things used to be better in some imagined bygone era. 'There's no point anymore' suggests that once upon a time things used to work, things used to change. Nostalgia is a disease in our politics. It is nothing more than a lie that we tell ourselves to make us feel better, or that we tell the younger generation to assert our wisdom and supremacy. It's bullshit. In my first election campaign I was out knocking on doors with my mother-in-law on the very council estate where she had lived as a child. An elderly woman came to her door and moaned that the area had gone to the dogs, that things used to be so much better, so much safer, and that she had no hope that I, as a politician, could or would do anything to change the situation. My mother-in-law, who had lived on this exact same street as a child, just a few doors down from this woman, pushed back with the best anti-nostalgia oration I have ever heard. She explained that at the age of twelve, while living on this street, she had got up every day before school to go to the local hotel to work in the kitchen and prepare the breakfasts for the guests; she would then head off to school for the day. After school she would be taken in a van to a pub car park a few miles away from her home where she was given sacks of potatoes to sell door to door, or on some occasions bags of sweets that she would be expected to flog in local pubs and clubs. She would get home after dark and the next morning she would start all over again. She scolded the woman and told her that, even though she did all this, she still had holes in her shoes, there was very little money to go around and her family were always in debt. In the intervening fifty years from her childhood to today, she said the world had changed dramatically and that her grandchildren would never need, or be allowed or expected, to do this. That the children growing up on these same streets today could focus entirely on their studies, and even the poorest kids were not doing the breakfast shift in the local cafes. The woman on the doorstep was dreaming of a 1960s idyll on this council estate, when things were better and life was easier, but my mother-in-law called out her misremembering of the facts.

Every one of the changes, all of the progress I have described here, was achieved by people expecting better and politics being the vehicle for that change. 'Nothing ever changes' is a cop-out! Those uttering the sentiment seem to see it as an act of defiance – it is in fact an act of capitulation and surrender. If nothing ever changes, what are you going to do about it? Moaning and not voting, or even protesting when grievance rather than solutions is your focus, will change absolutely nothing. 'Nothing ever changes' allows politicians to just crack on as they were. Even when things do so provably change with effort and campaigning, why would politicians bother to try to embody that model when people still say, 'Nothing ever changes'? Things did and do change: I can vote; you, most likely, get weekends off work and are entitled to weeks of holiday each year; I can decide what I do with my womb; your children no longer go up chimneys; my children were educated in newly built classrooms; you don't have to pay for a cast if you break your leg; I am entitled to equal pay; you don't have to put up with your hair stinking of cigarette smoke when you go out to a restaurant; I can request ten weeks off work to care for my loved ones; you are entitled to vaccines that ended global diseases in our country; I am entitled not to be raped in my marriage; you are entitled to freedom of expression that other global citizens dream of. Things do change!

So now that I have scolded you, dear reader, I shall turn to my own class of people to explain why 'nothing ever changes' has taken such a monumental hold over our politics. It would be crass to suggest that things have changed for anything but the worse of late. I feel I have moaned enough about that in this book already, but just to reiterate: in 2024 nothing fucking works! Many of those rights and entitlements I have highlighted have been degraded in reality. Yes, kids are not up chimneys, but hundreds of thousands of them are suffering from malnutrition. Yes, I am entitled not to be raped in my marriage, but good luck ever actually asserting that entitlement. My children's newly built classrooms are either crumbling because of the poor materials used or are pointless because there are not enough teachers to do any work in those classrooms. And, as for my womb, my gosh is there a global effort to take my decisions away.

The political class has failed to make hard-won changes mean things in people's lives, to seem like a change. Our country's National Health Service is probably one of the only examples of something that people actually value with gratitude and an understanding of where we would be without it. If you have ever tried to have a conversation with a conservative American about our socialised healthcare system you would be aghast at the attitude that healthcare is a privilege that should be paid for by the individual alone. Even the most conservative of ordinary Brits would never make such an argument. We show reverence to our NHS, sometimes to our detriment, but it is almost like a religion in our country to love the NHS. We feel so much less about our police services, our roads, our schools and our social security systems.

It feels as if nothing changes in our country because both politics and the people take a short-term view of history and a microscopic view of the future. 'What is the difference I feel right now?' is usually the only concern people have, along with 'What are you promising me will improve and do I believe you?' UK politics' inability to take a long-term view into the future and to bring people along with them is an utter curse that leads to masses of spending on short-term sticking plasters and promises written on leaflets. Promises that very well might be delivered for a year or two but do naff all to secure the future for your kids and grandkids. When the Victorians planned our railways and built the infrastructure that we still rely on today, someone in 1850 affected my daily life more than Rishi Sunak ever did. As PM, he delivered to me £37 off my monthly tax bill, which is great seeing as I was already paying over £300 more than I used to. He has also presided over the trains on that Victorian infrastructure going to absolute pot.

This is not a disease suffered by other countries. My husband's current doom-mongering Cassandra cry to me, his politician wife, is about chip manufacture. Not the kind you eat – the kind you definitely relied on to be reading the text in front of you. Even if you are old-school and are reading it in actual book format, I wrote it on a computer, it was printed using one, sold to you using one, and the lights and infrastructure you depend on to see it are undoubtedly relying on chips of some variety or another. We bang on about energy security all the time, worried that we will only be saved from hypothermia in our cold and rainy land if we rely on Russian gas and Saudi oil. We don't want to be beholden to oligarchs and despots who could just switch off our lights and our boilers, but we have seemingly not worried too much about the future and the fact that the thing all of our infrastructure relies on is made somewhere else entirely and we could be left begging them for access, willing to give over anything just to use our smartphones. Luckily for us, Taiwan – yes, that is Taiwan, not Chinese Taipei – is the global leader in chip manufacture. We are pretty pally with Taiwan. Let's pray that this remains the case. I am not saying any of this in order to start some sort of global schism; I am saying it in praise of Taiwan, who over the last few decades thought about the future of their frankly quite insecure country and hoovered up pretty much all of the brainpower and manufacturing nous in chip manufacture. They are the Victorian industrialists of our day. Taiwan accounts for 90 per cent of the world's microchip manufacture. Thank Taiwan that you can read this book; they had more to do with getting it to you than I did.

You didn't pick up this book to read someone who is

quite frankly not informed enough about microchips* or Taiwan do a deep-dive into why Taiwan's politics have secured it this future, but it would be remiss of me not to mention that it is in no small part due to their relative insecurity in the shadow of a Chinese superpower: their politicians needed something that would provide security not just in domestic economics but also in global politics. It's all politics, my friends.

Perhaps long-term views and future planning rely on relative insecurity on the part of your nation. Maybe like people who triumph after hitting rock bottom, here in the UK we have not had a rock bottom recently. After all, we did create the entire welfare state and healthcare system we depend on in the aftermath of the Second World War. Maybe calamity is the greatest driver in things actually changing.

There is, of course, no maybe about it, and Covid-19 taught this to the world. 'Nothing ever changes' was truly challenged as a belief system here in the UK, as with most countries around the world, when everything changed overnight. I don't need to tell you what that looked like because you were there. It isn't just that in the face of a mortal threat everyone's individual life was changed; it was that

---

* I would like to take a moment to thank my husband, without whom I would be even more of a tech dunce. When anyone talks about tech in politics, I ring him and make him explain it to me. Him explaining blockchain to me should have been filmed and turned into a comedy sketch. When Jeremy Hunt mentioned quantum computing in the budget, I called my husband for a briefing and he said to me, 'Jess, don't worry about it, it actually doesn't exist, and what the chancellor announced today was so paltry that there is no way the UK will be a player in this field.'

for the first time in my lifetime I saw how political wisdom and practice changed. Suddenly anything was possible.

There is absolutely nothing I have tried to change in the decade I have been an elected representative where I haven't been pushed back with a million reasons why the thing I want is not possible. Ask for better policies at work to end sexual harassment and you will be told: it will be too onerous on businesses to manage the regulation. Sorry, love, not possible. Ask that it be made a statutory requirement for all public bodies that fund frontline support services for citizens to fund specialist support for victims of abuse and violence and you will be told: it is not possible to insist that local mental health services should have a women's abuse service, because they have to decide based on their own populations what is best. I mean, I would love to find a local mental health trust with a population to serve that has no victims of rape in it – really, what nirvana have they created? But the answer is the same: sorry, love, not possible. Ask that any welfare benefit change doesn't make victims of domestic abuse less safe, and you will be told: it cannot be done because it is too complicated to change the system for individual groups. Sorry, love, not possible. Governments have to say that things are not possible because they don't want to say the truth, which is actually: 'Oh, we don't give a shit about this, please go away.' I would honestly much prefer this; I know where I am with a solid 'fuck off moaning about this'. It's what I expect in my real life from my friends and loved ones. I am grateful for their honesty.

The sentence I utter in politics more than anything else in the face of this pushback is: 'They put a man on the moon and brought him back twelve years before I was born, I think perhaps we could manage to make it so every police force in the country has a dedicated rape and sexual violence unit.' Are we so useless that we cannot think of a way around bureaucracy or the way things have always been done to find actual solutions to our nation's problems, or are we just so unambitious that we don't try? Nostalgia for the way things have always been done in parliament is like a cancer. Thank God we had a better attitude towards cancer, otherwise we would have just said, 'Yeah, people die of cancer. That sucks, doesn't it? Never mind.'

We did not do this in the pandemic. We gave it the moonshot treatment. We showed that things we never thought would be possible were in fact completely possible and we moved the legislation to make them happen at breakneck speed. We got every homeless person off the streets, we produced systems that fed a nation, we created hundreds of new refuge beds for victims fleeing domestic abuse. For goodness sake, we basically invented a universal basic income through the furlough scheme. Millions more people than ever before were able to access our welfare system, damning all the pushbacks I had previously heard for why the system could never be changed. We turned conference centres and airport hangars into hospitals. We put up tents in every neighbourhood and filed people through to receive vaccines, which, had we tried to create them before the pandemic (if only we had), would have taken decades of bureaucracy and penny-pinching, essentially stopping progress, and we would never have had the roll-out so universally allowed.

In short – we made shit happen. It wasn't just the politicians, they created the fertile ground for innovation through will and resources, but the response to the Covid-19 pandemic relied on everyone in our country, every institution, everyone's goodwill and compliance, people's individual efforts to do their bit. No decent person in the country thought that they didn't have to play their part, take on something new, fight hard for this group or that group. For the first time in my political life, I watched a nation of people properly recognising their own privilege and seeking what they had for others. They wouldn't have seen it in these terms, but everyone said things like, 'Yes, I know it's hard for me, I miss my family, but at least I have a garden for the kids to run around in' or, '. . . at least my job is secure' or, '. . . at least my kids have a computer' or, '. . . at least I am not living with an abuser'. People fought for those with less than them in what I truly believe is our nation's actual character – not the one we are presented with in newspapers or on social media, where it would appear that we all absolutely fucking hate our neighbours, think poor people are feckless and deserve hanging.

The public did another thing that bucks against some of what I have asserted in this book. They accepted wholeheartedly with kindness and analysis that the politics of the situation was not going to be perfect. They were so lovingly grateful for what they had, or what they had been given in the crisis, that they didn't mind mistakes being made or directions changed. They assumed good faith in those making the decisions and understood that it was incredibly hard. The amount of slack the government were being cut when they were making mistakes was at times infuriating to me. When we couldn't get enough PPE for our local care homes, or tests targeted at healthcare workers, my ability to put pressure on the government to do this better was definitely affected by a general view that people were doing their best. On reflection I find this charming; at the time I wanted to scream a bit. I really rely on public outrage to move the dial on things, and it was pretty hard to make arguments that enough wasn't being done in various areas without the assistance of the public.

What a shame then that this good faith was eventually entirely squandered by the politicians who had been given so much slack. The partying and lying and the bunging of contracts to friends in a gold rush for disaster capitalists left the public feeling betrayed, their own trust in good character misplaced. The fact that, while they were looking for reasons to forgive, others were looking for opportunities to get rich doesn't make having good faith in politics an easy sell thereafter.

I am not saying for one second that the actions taken during the pandemic were all good, or that the breakneck speed of decisions was always reliable. They weren't. Too few of us, myself included, gave anywhere near enough thought to what the educational and mental health implications for our nation's children, including my own, would be. If I'd known then what I know now about this I would definitely have made different decisions, pushed more for services to be put in place to manage this issue. One of the problems was that, when the initial calamity began to abate, the government got rid of the 'can-do' attitude and reverted to saying, 'Sorry, love, it's not possible' once again. There was a really good strategy outlined to provide help with children's catch-up, both educational and emotional, and the government asked for it to be written up, but when it was, they just decided it couldn't be done. What children were offered in tutoring and support after the lockdown cannot be described as a slingshot let alone a moonshot.

This yet again speaks of an inability in politics to think about the future rather than the immediate. Even though the pandemic did show how many things were totally possible where previously you would have been laughed at for suggesting them, it was all happening in real time – what matters now today, not what do we want for our country in the future? Where is our moonshot for the future? Where is our Taiwan? The only people who thought about securing a future in the pandemic were the Michelle Mones of this world, who were imagining the yachts they might buy when travel was allowed and how they might get a nice little contract to secure them.

Money is a problem, of course, and I can already see some of my colleagues rolling their eyes at some of what I am saying. The Covid-19 pandemic cost our country trillions. Trillions of pounds that have left us with debt interest payments that are more than we currently spend on education. I am not an idiot who doesn't recognise this fairly pertinent fact: that, if money was no object, of course we could pay everyone's wages, send out laptops to every schoolchild, draft in thousands of new NHS staff and increase the number of police on our streets. The pandemic presented a specific challenge in that it was hard to raise money from it (unless you were Matt Hancock's pub landlord-cum-PPE entrepreneur) and easy to spend it. This will obviously not always be the case with other government policies. We need, for example, to have a very serious conversation in this country about how we all as individuals pay for social care if we want, as I do, for it to be free at the point of delivery. If we want to see that changed, we are going to have to pay for it, which, by the way, most people already do one way or another, this is not a new cost. Personally, I would rather pay a new form of national insurance than have to sell my home or for the standard of care to be determined by how much family wealth I have. That's just me, just my personal opinion, and one I know will not be shared by all, but solutions need to be found and risks need to be taken.

The truth is, when it comes to money to pay for changes to happen, there is always going to be an element of up-front cost for the potential to save money in the future by solving a public ill, or to make money in the future because of initial investments made. I'm betting Taiwanese politicians are pretty chuffed at the return on their initial capital investment in what was formerly United Micro-electronics Corporation, and additional investment in

1987 in what was by then TSCM, which would become the world's largest chip manufacturer. It doesn't end there: Taiwan has offered financial incentives to encourage chip manufacturers to invest in facilities and new technologies, passing legislation to let companies flip research and development costs into tax credits. I really want to make a lame joke about when the chips were down the Taiwanese government won, but that would be too droll. We shouldn't always just see money as a barrier, or even as an excuse for not trying to change things. We will not change things without the funds to do it, but in reality money can always be found; political will, long-term thinking and proper planning are what is actually in short supply.

We are not a country with masses of oil or gas – no matter how much I dig up my garden, I am not going to find the cobalt required to make our country rich in natural resources. We do have a lot of weather and should sweat that asset as we head towards a greener future. But we cannot rely simply on a stroke of good geological luck; we are going to need to use our brains, our existing wealth, our standing and our will.

One of the reasons people feel as if nothing changes is because, even when we are rich or are winning some global race in some industry or another, it doesn't feel as if that wealth is properly shared around. Yes, the country doing well always means public services will improve as tax revenues rise, and arguably, or at least in theory, we have enough labour laws in this country to ensure that if an industry is thriving then so too will the wages of its workers. However, it does seem to most people that while someone gets monumentally rich, the little guy never prospers. The Post Office subpostmasters scandal speaks to the nation's strength of feeling on these matters. While Fujitsu, the private company, made millions from their broken computer system, the little guy literally paid the price. Money invested by the state into private companies in order for them to become more profitable is absolutely what should happen, but it cannot be a no-strings-attached affair, there has to be a built-in public good. After all, it is ultimately *our* money. The levers the government could pull using investment could solve all sorts of public ills. When companies were given what can only be described as a gazillion pounds to build High Speed Rail, they could have absolutely demanded that the workforce had to have a certain wage level and that half of them had to be women. When governments put masses of investment into green industries or train companies to ensure that the thing actually happens, why on earth would we not expect to see some form of advanced return on our money – literally money back into the exchequer other than through economic growth increasing tax takes. We end up having to windfall big oil and gas giants to do this after the fact rather than designing it in. There should definitely have been some strings attached to the projects commissioned with masses of wasted money during the pandemic.

The political catastrophe in Westminster that happened after the pandemic, where on some days the nation literally had more prime ministers than hot dinners, meant that

that spirit of ingenuity, that push to break boundaries, that sweeping the deck of excuses and making things possible didn't lead to the political change it could have. But there has certainly been huge cultural change in our country: we have a school attendance crisis post-pandemic and levels of long-term sickness that are costing our nation billions.

I recognise for some this sounds a bit like I am missing Boris Johnson and his can-do attitude, or suggesting that if Westminster had just kept him rather than descending into a Conservative Party soap opera things might have been better. That is not at all what I am saying; he caused the immediate rot of good faith with his actions and his subsequent lies. If he had cared more about the people and the possibilities than he did about protecting himself, he wouldn't have lied; he would have told the truth and probably survived, people were in a forgiving mood. He thought only about playing the game in front of him at the time without an eye to the future. He was not capable of actually turning a genuine crisis into decades of renewal because he could only think from minute to minute as he started to panic about himself.

The fact that he was replaced by Liz Truss, who herself is now trying to make out like it was all bureaucrats and shadowy institutions who stopped her in her tracks, should also not be confused with what I am saying. Yes, bureaucracy and sometimes regulation does slow things down, but ultimately it is the responsibility of the politicians to show political will to change something and have a workable plan for the future to do that. Liz Truss had a sledgehammer and a plan that, if written down, wouldn't cover one side of a Rizla paper.*

'Nothing ever changes' is provably untrue; stuff absolutely does change, both for the better and the worse, but for too long the public have been able to say nothing changes with complete conviction and feel that they are being proven right. Very little changed for the better under fourteen years of Conservative government,† aside from the fact that gay people can now get married rather than just have a civil partnership (although they can't do it in a church), which is literally all I can point to in terms of progress forward rather than back. They extended some things created by the last Labour government, such as free nursery places, the weekly allowance for which has increased from fifteen to thirty hours. But that isn't change, it is development, natural progression, and not every child is entitled to it, unlike the original fifteen hours. Hardly worthy of a ticker-tape parade.

'Nothing ever changes' is not uttered in Westminster by our politicians, but we have definitely been guilty of falling for the line that it is too hard to change the status quo and of trying to tinker with things as they are, thinking we'll worry about tomorrow tomorrow. Some of this comes

---

* My husband wrote his last will and testament on a Rizla as a teenager, which shows how many assets he had to worry about. It was more that he wished to be disposed of in a wheelie bin in our local park. This is a poor plan and would never be able to happen, much like Liz Truss's plans for the economy.

† Clue's in the name, guys. They are not trying to hide that they don't want to change things; they want to conserve them as they are.

from the media environment of the day; there is always some bloody crisis or salacious scandal to distract us, like a kitten with a ball of string. The only way we will stop people thinking that nothing ever changes is if we start to actually come up with real radical changes we want to see for the future, not just for today, and if the public take part, just as they did with Covid, in both making and allowing that to happen.

So, what would that look like? Let's put a can-do Covid-19 approach to the test and see.

7

How It Should Work

Shamelessly, I am going to use the example I know the most about to show how politics could and should be done, if we were to take the same can-do attitude to public policy as we took during the Covid-19 pandemic: men's violence and abuse of women and children. Even more shamelessly, I will use the commitment made by the Labour Party as my guide. I do really try when writing about politics not to be boring and just blether on, repeating hackneyed Labour Party lines. I think one of the worst things about politics today is that most of the public interaction with our politicians is through news interviews where they have been trained to stick religiously to a party political line rather than answering the bleedin' question that they were asked. Why anyone thinks that this endears us to the public is beyond me, but someone has probably written a book that proves me entirely wrong. I don't really care; I know what I think and that is:

'Answer the goddamn question!'* However, I happen to think that the Labour Party's commitment in the space of violence against women and girls is pretty good, probably because I was one of the people who wrote it.

The Labour Party has committed to halving the incidence of violence against women and girls in a decade. To the casual observer this might seem a bit lame; you might very well think it unambitious to only ask for it to be halved when we should be striving for it to be eliminated. No shit, Sherlock – let's deal in reality not fantasy. The only thing we would do if we committed to ending it is to fail and have no one believe that we were in the slightest bit serious about changing a social ill that is literally as old as time if we stood up and claimed we could stop it altogether. Might as well stand up and say I want world peace and then sing 'Land of the Free'.

This commitment is off-the-charts ambitious. It irritates me a little bit when people say that the Labour Party is not being bold enough; only a little bit because, well, I agree sometimes. However, the blanket view that it isn't promising big change ignores this and other commitments that would be absolute game-changers if they were achieved. The first reason I will defend the party is because it passes the test I have set about being future-focused. Tick. However, for it to be truly rooted in the future it cannot just seek to do a good job through the public services it may manage for a period of ten years; it must fundamentally

---

* To be fair to my people, we do get asked some properly stupid bloody questions. I still try to answer them but I point out that it is a stupid question.

change the institutions at play to ensure that its efforts cannot be undone, so that the following ten years can sign up to halve the incidence of violence against women and girls again. Saying you have a plan for the future is not the same as actually future-proofing it.

I have been known to rave endlessly about how much the last Labour government provided for my family and it surely did. I was given free childcare and tax credits, and my husband and I both had good, stable public sector jobs. My children were given trust funds by the government, who didn't think it was only kids called St John de Pfeffel-Montague who should be provided with a nest egg when they turned eighteen. So, when my kid turned eighteen last year and he had nine grand thanks to the luck of his birth under a Labour government, I was reminded of how things were and could be again. Mind you, the last time I saw Tony Blair I told him that if my son buys a motorbike with that money, I will come for the last Blair government. So far, he has put it in a long-term savings account to help him buy a house in the future and he lent some of it to me: when Liz Truss's government pushed our mortgage rates so high we – yes, even families as affluent as mine – struggled to make ends meet. My kids and I were supported by Sure Start centres; I was given mandated time off work to care for my dying mother, because the last Labour government recognised that workers lose their jobs when they have to undertake caring responsibilities. They did so much for my family that we were able to thrive. The trouble with a lot of what they did was that it wasn't locked up with enough padlocks to protect it into the future. The children's centre I went to is now closed down, the tax credits we were entitled to are gone, the council contracts of public service that employed both my husband and me vanished. Some of the progress was way too easy to undo. Childcare remained because it would have been too politically toxic to get rid of even in a time of austerity, but pretty much all the policies that meant my family progressed and thrived to the point where we give way more back in both tax and time to society today have been obliterated. To make politics and policy actually benefit for the long term you need to future-proof.

It might sound like electioneering that the Labour Party has this numerical target to halve the incidence of men's violence against women and girls, but I will defend it being spoken about in these terms. I never trust politics that makes bland promises and, if I had a pound for every time I have heard a politician claim that they will do 'everything they can' to end some social ill without putting a plan forward or a metric for measurement on it, well, I would be able to fund women's refuges for the rest of time. I am so fucking sick of hearing platitudes like 'enough is enough' and 'lessons will be learned' when there's some tragedy like 72 people burning to death in a tower block, or a known sexual predator becomes a policeman and then rapes and kills a woman. Bullshit will enough be enough; they are simply saying it to get through a difficult interview on their department or council's abject failure. The day after they have said enough is enough, they will move on, and nothing will change. If you ever hear a politician utter these words again, I want you to pen them an email that says:

> Dear Platitude Spouter, can you please give me some details about how exactly you are going to change this in the future? I would appreciate seeing a detailed plan with some timeframes attached.
>
> Best wishes from a constituent who is bored of your pointless rhetoric.

I think having targets and timeframes built into any pledge that is made is not only polite, it shows that you actually are expecting to be held accountable for what you have said. Rishi Sunak promised the UK public that he would reduce waiting lists in the NHS; he would have achieved this promise if he had reduced them by one, leaving another million people languishing on the list while their hip hurt and they were getting slowly sicker. The funny (not funny really) fact is that, even though he failed to tell us by how much he would reduce waiting lists or by when, he was giving himself an easy task that he could later crow about and he couldn't even manage that. Waiting lists went up.

Using the efforts made during the pandemic as a guide to how it should be done, we saw how heaven and earth could be moved to ensure that everyone had access to at least one vaccine by a certain date; and eventually there were expectations matched by targets about the number of tests available and how quickly people should be able to get them. The latter was admittedly chaotic initially and Matt Hancock was definitely cherry-picking data that made him look good, but the fundamental point was that there was a numerical measurement and a national expectation of a service level, and the government knew they had to sweat every asset they had to achieve it.

We count what we care about, the numbers matter. So, how will we do this measurable task I am talking about? The very first thing that needs to be truly dealt with in this space is the data. Boring, I know, but we just do not have reliable data on the number of incidents of domestic abuse, sexual violence, exploitation, stalking and all the other forms this violence takes. It's no good in politics having a commitment that you can just fudge with the way you count things. That is only of any value to politicians trying to win elections and makes precious little difference to the people in our country. For the worst example of this, see how the Conservative government sought to change the way we count child poverty by looking at new metrics on workless households, for example, rather than just focusing on the number of children who lived in relative or abject poverty. They claimed it was because those figures didn't give a full picture, but it looked very like searching for a tiny good news story from the data that actually showed child poverty soaring. I mean, I wouldn't want to look as though I was starving children so I would try not to, rather than playing around with numbers.

When it comes to the kind of violence and abuse I am concerned with, we rely on a variety of data sources, from police data, data collected by the Office for National Statistics and other department data, such as homelessness caused by domestic abuse and child protection plans where abuse is a factor. It's a bit of a mess, to be honest, and even if all agencies, such as healthcare providers, did have a single flag on domestic abuse, it would be a massive underrepresentation. This isn't like diabetes; people hide this stuff.

The target I am working towards is to halve the incidence. The most important word there is 'incidence' because so much of the abuse and violence suffered by women and children in our country is repeat offences. The truth is that, if a woman who had been beaten by her husband came forward the first time and received all of the correct social and criminal interventions in order for it never to happen again, well, then, my work would be done. I wouldn't just halve domestic abuse, I could end it. The reason she doesn't come forward the first time is because she believes nothing will be done to help her; she is, as things stand, very sadly not wrong. The reason she comes forward on the second, third or even thirty-seventh time it happens is because she is so scared for her life, she has no choice but to rely on the system. When she receives a woeful service that disbelieves her and says she doesn't have enough evidence to prove anything bad happened; when she is told that there isn't a safe house for her to move to and that, in speaking up, she will be reported to social services as she is not keeping her children safe; and when, to cap it all, she will receive no money from our welfare system for six weeks if she kicks out the person she relies on entirely for finances – this is the reason she doesn't come back and try again the next time she takes a beating. She has now learned that what she suspected, and what her perpetrator told her about no one helping her, was absolutely true. Next time she might die.

Getting a proper baseline of the data on the incidence of domestic and sexual abuse is going to be vitally important to ensure that the target doesn't just rely on police data – most women don't come forward to the police. Most women come forward to a health service provider, a nurse, doctor or midwife. If we were to look at police data alone, we would be missing absolutely loads of issues and, what is more, the government recently messed around with the way that police record instances of domestic abuse. The Home Office introduced new rules in June 2023, telling police to only count one crime for each time a victim comes forward, thus allowing police to count fewer crimes of threatening or abusive messages. When crime figures were released after this change had been made, they showed that domestic abuse-related crime fell by 23,000 cases compared to the same period the previous year and public order offences with a domestic abuse flag were down by 24 per cent, a reduction of almost 3,000 when comparing July–September 2023 to the previous year.* They didn't reduce domestic abuse at all through work or effort; they just stopped counting thousands of incidents so it could look like they had done a good job. This is pure politics,

---

* This data comes from the independent Commissioner for Domestic Abuse for England and Wales.

and if I wanted to find something wrong with politics this would be pretty close to the top of the list. Counting wrong is not interpretation – it is lying, plain and simple.

In this brilliant world I am imagining where we are doing politics right, we should commit to a goal; it should have a workable target and that target must be monitored against data sets that can actually be trusted. We need to invest in proper data gathering and research into what is the best way to monitor public policy and check whether it is working. One of the real overlooked tragedies of the years of austerity has been how backroom staff working on data and analysis in our public services were hollowed out in efficiency cuts. Take the police, for example: thousands of civilian staff who worked on this exact thing were cleared out when budgets were cut. Staff who dealt with forensics, trends and analysis were burned on the bonfire because the politically expedient thing to do was keep uniformed police officers that the public see but hollow out all of the things that those officers rely on to make improvements in how they do their job. This stops change from happening and leaves frontline staff less capable of doing anything but mopping up problems.

Some people hate targets in politics, and I have definitely seen cases where the target was hit but the point was missed. Take, for example, the Sunak government's commitment to cut waiting lists in the NHS. All the effort to achieve this was about getting people through the blocked-up system so it could crow about a number rather than also allowing the space to think about why there were so many people on the waiting list in the first place. On a visit to my local hospital during the push for reduced lists, the chief executive told me that every week he had government officials breathing down his neck about surgery waiting list targets, but no one was focused on the fact that we waste millions of pounds amputating the limbs of people with diabetes because their condition was spotted too late, or poorly managed. That particular target, on the face of it, does seem to put more onus on chopping people's legs off quickly rather than on saving them. Not sure I'd want my leg whipped off so Rishi Sunak can say he stuck to his target.

That said, I have found that, in politics, if we are not counting properly then we are simply not that bothered about the outcome we are claiming we want to achieve. Data and targets are really important. For example, there is no government data kept and studied relating to the number of women murdered by men each year. That data is collected, collated and analysed by volunteers and academics who care about it. Those volunteers don't have the levers of data collection that governments do, so just as one example I cannot tell you how many of the women who were killed last year were refugees to this country. I cannot tell you accurately how many times each of the women killed had interacted with services, seeking help. We can do endless amounts of reading and research into the individual cases and try as best we can to build a picture of trends and recommendations – and all power to the Femicide Census for doing amazing work in this space – but it is unforgivable that I cannot just ask the UK Home Office for a specific data set about the women murdered and receive it. They wouldn't have the first clue; believe me, I've tried.

If we are to do politics well, we need good data and we need to be honest about what that data says even when it is politically unpalatable for those of us trying to change things. I promise you now that if I do ever get a chance to do any of this work in government, and even if I was given all the resource in the world (I won't be) in the first five years, do not expect to see dramatic downturns in the number of incidents of abuse and violence. On some occasions the data is going to show increases in this abuse and not just because of specific events. For example, all of Dr Harold Shipman's murders featured in the homicide data for one year even though the UK's worst ever serial killer had been killing people for years. That would have made that year look pretty gruesome and would allow a government the following year to proclaim that they had halved the murder rate. Leaving aside murderous anomalies such as this, though, it is important and good politics to always just be honest about the data. If rape charging, for example, was one of the metrics I was using within the overarching target and it started to fall dramatically regardless of efforts to increase it, politicians should be willing to accept that situation, look at what they are doing that might have caused it and seek to course-correct. Just putting a bow on the data you like is no use nor ornament. Remember, in this thought experiment we are trying to solve a problem not win in a tricky interview on Sky News.

Let's assume now that we have a good and reliable data set that we have agreed as the baseline for action. We have to roll the pitch in order to get the public, and the institutions who will actually have to do the work, on board. There is a reason to be cheerful here – the public are already with me on this one. Seems like a small thing to say that the general public don't like abuse and violence; well, it isn't. Two decades ago, when I started this work, awareness and sympathy for victims of domestic abuse was relatively bad. It was certainly not the political issue it is today and, as a society, we tolerated way more violence against women than we would today. Don't get me wrong, we have a long way to go in how attitudes need to shift; for example, in the case of adult victims of sexual exploitation. A decade ago, using the term 'child prostitute' was regular in policy terms; the uncovering of wide-scale child sexual exploitation in this era has done much to stop us blaming girls for what were considered to be risky behaviours once upon a time. Today we keep these poor attitudes for adult women who are sexually exploited. We ignore the fact that most of the women sold for sex in our country started being exploited in childhood, and we think there is something magical that happens to them on their eighteenth birthday where all their childhood trauma, all the men who have abused them over their lives and all of their mental ill health and reliance on substances are not factors in their 'decision' to sell blowjobs for a tenner. We think these women are acting out of choice and that a nice, healthy, civilised society should tolerate this as a choice. Sure, not a choice you would make for yourself or your daughter, but you are not one of 'those' women.*

Attitudes and how policy changes them have a long way to go in this space, but I do not think for a second that making this issue a political centrepiece is something that will be a particularly hard sell. One of the pushbacks policymakers often get when trying to change things is that legislation doesn't change culture and culture eats policy for breakfast. Basically, you can write whatever law you want but if the people are not behind it then you will not succeed. Well, in the space of men's violence against women the opposite has happened. The public are in a better place than the policymakers. Where the public have cared more and more about this, and where women have for a decade now marched and demanded better, only the tiniest piecemeal changes have been made. So, we have won this particular culture war, and like all culture wars, it has delivered next to nothing.

The trouble is, this is a massive volume issue; it will literally take a moonshot effort to do something about it – it is an actual pandemic. To really do the work that is needed, the institutions involved, which have plenty of other functions, have to be prepared to prioritise it in their

---

* There are few things I find more maddening about the liberal left than the push for us to not tolerate or promote capitalism of any kind except the one that sells women's bodies. It is literally trendy to support the sexual exploitation of adults.

actions, not merely in their words. This pitch-rolling is considerably harder.

The police as an institution – who are currently, rightly or wrongly, the leading agency involved in domestic and sexual abuse – cannot, if we are actually to change this thing, just keep on spouting the line that violence against women and girls is a priority for them. It is just not true. Never has been, never will be if this culture doesn't change. Eighteen per cent of all call-outs to the police are domestic abuse related. Ignoring child abuse, sexual violence and human trafficking for a moment, stop to consider that nearly one in every five calls to the police each day is *just* domestic abuse. If you were to take a basic view of resources alone and look at a local police force where this 18 per cent statistic applied (it's an average; some will be more, some less), you might assume that 18 per cent of the budget of that police force would be spent on the policing of domestic abuse. Wrong! Not a chance in hell. Okay, so that would be a rudimentary test and, as I have explained throughout this book, things are much more complicated than that. You might assume, though, that there would be a specific department in this local constabulary just for domestic abuse, what with it being such a priority for said police force. Well, if there is, I've never seen one. Most police forces in the country have a section called a public protection unit (PPU). PPUs deal with all crime-related violence and abuse of both adults and children, men and women alike. I genuinely couldn't find a more up-to-date description of what my local police force's PPU does than this one from the Office for the West Midlands Police and Crime Commissioner in 2014, but here it is:

> Its areas of responsibility include child abuse investigation and safeguarding, child sexual exploitation including online activity, the investigation of all rape and serious sexual offences, aspects of human trafficking, high-risk domestic abuse investigation and safeguarding as well as vulnerable adult abuse investigation and safeguarding. The department is also responsible for the management of registered sex offenders as well as the preparation of Internal Management Reviews as part of the Serious Case Review/Domestic Homicide Review processes.

If domestic abuse represents 18 per cent, add in all this other stuff and we will be dealing with at least a quarter of all policing activity in the West Midlands. Do we think a quarter of the entire West Midlands Police budget is spent on the PPU? Alas, this is not how budget data (that pesky data again) is broken down, so there is no way of knowing, but when I recently supported a woman reporting high-risk domestic abuse and rape in Birmingham, the second-largest city in the country, the detective in the case told me he was one of only two detectives in his team. Two!

There is no way to reduce the incidence of violence against women and girls without every police force in the country actually prioritising it with more than just words in an annual review document. The pitch needs to be rolled with this and many other institutions. It would very much be the best practice in politics for a government department to lead from the front on this issue and hope that every police force in the country would get that their individual progression and standing should take account of it, meaning they would start to be better, spend more, allocate time and money in better police responses both to victims and to actual offender management for the perpetrators. Hope springs eternal. I am afraid to say that when change is what we are after, sometimes force is the only way. Asking nicely hasn't worked; we should stop hoping for better and just make demands using laws to ensure that this happens. Less pitch-rolling than forcing people to actually get on the pitch.

I totally buy into the idea that individual chief constables and individual police forces have to be allowed to allocate their resources as they see fit. The needs in a city like Birmingham cannot be compared to those in Devon, for example. I don't know, perhaps Devon is an absolute hotspot for gang violence or needs a counter-terror unit, but I don't think so. Of course, police forces across the country cannot have a prescribed way of working. However, the last time I looked, there isn't a part of the country that has no women in it. Even the Isle of Man has women. Domestic abuse, like burglary, is a constant in every place. I am beyond waiting for police forces to prioritise this issue – I am afraid political force is the only answer. For me, that looks like a women's safety unit in every police force area, which is resourced at least nearing the level of crime domestic abuse creates in that area. It should absolutely not be staffed only by police officers but also by experts in the field of domestic abuse and those who have worked for years with both the victims and the perpetrators.

By comparison, what I have been offered, in nine years of asking the Home Office under the Tories to do something about this, is a promise that more police training will happen. Seriously, shoot me if I ever think that police officers attending a training course is enough to change the culture of domestic and sexual abuse policing in our country. The *Guardian* reported after a freedom of information request in 2022 that 'nine police forces had not given any officers specialist domestic abuse training by the end of 2021, and that those which had, in most cases, had only trained small numbers'. Only one police force area surveyed said that all officers in their force were trained in domestic abuse. Some priority!

As I have already said, be careful what you are grateful for, and even if the government were now to announce that every officer in the country must have specialist domestic abuse training it would in the long run just become a tickbox exercise. We would hit the target and miss the point. Frankly, it is the bare fucking minimum!

The other thing that police forces would have to change in my fantasised nirvana is that they would actually have to do some offender management of the most violent and dangerous perpetrators. Imagine that on your street there is someone who has in the past committed a terrorism offence – let's say a low-level one; they have shared terrorism propaganda online, they were caught and charged and went to prison for a couple of years. Rightly, you can expect that through both overt and covert policing that person and their activities will be monitored by counter-terror units until such time as they are considered to no longer be a risk to society. Good stuff, that makes me feel safer – dangerous people are monitored and interrupted in their harmful behaviours. Who could argue with that?

Now, on your street living opposite your would-be terrorist is a man, and I am going to be truly extreme here to make my point: he was a known domestic abuser although never charged in his first relationship, but in his second he ended up in prison for the murder of his wife. This fella was released from prison, where he served eighteen years for his crimes. You see, he murdered her at home with a kitchen knife so the minimum sentence for that is fifteen years; if he had murdered a stranger on the street with the exact same knife, the minimum sentence would be twenty-five years, because, well ... we don't think murder in homes (usually of women) is as bad. I digress in anger. Do you think the same overt and covert police monitoring tactics are being used against this man, who is clearly a danger to society given the string of women he has abused and harmed? Well, you, my friend, would be completely wrong if you thought so. Sure, he had a probation officer when he came out of prison to help him rehabilitate, and the local police know where he lives; he will have conditions put on him, although in my experience such conditions are rarely policed with any urgency, like in the killing of Zara Aleena: her murder took place two days after her murderer had been recalled to prison for not attending his probation. The man who killed her had, in separate known incidents, tried to assault a 12-year-old girl; throttled, slapped and pushed an ex-girlfriend down the stairs, and punched and hit another former partner. When the police failed to recall him to prison because he had breached his release conditions, he had twenty-eight previous convictions for sixty-nine separate offences. So, as we can see, the conditions are not particularly urgently policed. Sadly, too many women like Cherylee Shennan are killed by men who have killed women before. Paul O'Hara, who murdered Cherylee, had already served a life sentence in prison for killing a previous girlfriend. Clearly, great monitoring and offender management were not happening in his case and, guess what, he hurt more women.

I have been extreme and spoken about cases of murder to make a point. But if a situation where a man kills his wife and then is given the opportunity to murder a future partner can happen, imagine how many of the most violent and dangerous rapists and domestic abusers who don't (usually by luck) end up killing anyone are able to repeat offend again and again against multiple women and children. No one in the community is monitoring this. We just accept it.

The truth about this issue is that the volume is simply too much. Women are too abused for the existing policing levels in this country to be able to manage the numbers. There are a lot fewer terrorists than there are domestic abusers. It would take so much more resource than is available to manage even the *convicted* violent offenders, who account for at most 10 per cent of the actually dangerous repeat offenders because hardly anyone is convicted. We are talking of the need for thousands and thousands of extra police and probation officers, whose only job is offender monitoring and management.

The good politics model I am proposing means being honest about that, facing it head-on and working towards implementing a system that is actually achievable. The absolute truth, which no politician would dare to say, is we literally cannot manage the levels of this abuse quickly, so we are going to have to do much less than we would want and that does mean that some cases will be missed. That is the truth, and we should be brave enough to say it rather than pretending we are some trailblazing, world-beating superheroes who have all the solutions. I really, really care about this subject and not even if I was given unlimited resources could I deliver anything remotely world-beating quickly. What a politician should be given the space to say is that it won't be perfect but at the very least we should seek to design a system of offender management and monitoring that is better than before. We should use techniques practised by anti-terror policing to try to identify in every police force area a rolling list of the most dangerous men in our communities and ensure that they are being monitored and engaged in diversion and rehabilitation. It is important for me to say that I believe in offender rehabilitation; however, there are undoubtedly cases of sexual predators and domestic abusers so violent that they cannot be rehabilitated so they will just have to be constantly monitored or incarcerated.

It would be easy for me to dodge here the issue of financing this operation. If we were (we won't) ever to have enough offender managers in either the police or probation service to enable those doing the work to have a safe and actually workable caseload (say, ten offenders each off the top of my head) we would need hundreds of thousands more staff, loads of investment in tech solutions for data gathering, monitoring and analysis, and some pretty robust investment in external projects run by the voluntary sector to support both victims and perpetrators through the scheme. It would not be cheap and is (thanks to the shocking state of the public finances and debt rates) not affordable as things stand. Might as well be honest about that. Just a small aside to say that the predicted cost to the country of the failed Rwanda deportation scheme, which at most will send 300 people (lol – it will never send even a full small planeload), is £576.8 million, so half a billion quid for a total waste of time – £1.92 million per asylum seeker! It's not just our public finances that stop us investing in stuff; it is also the choices we make and, as of late, we've been making bad ones.

Back to the point, the honest truth is that this stuff is expensive, and we have to decide as a nation if we want to spend the money on it. Covid was, as the comparator, something we all pretty much signed up to getting into debt for as a nation and we have continued to cut the government quite a lot of slack for the eye-watering debt levels it created. Obviously, what I am suggesting has an economic growth element to it, as it would create thousands of fairly well-paid skilled jobs and would ultimately increase the tax take as a result, but it would have to be paid for up front. In pretty much every interview we give, Labour politicians are asked: 'How are you going to pay for this?' The Tory government were not so robustly challenged because the Conservatives had (regardless of soaring debt levels and an economy in recession) succeeded in landing the idea that the Labour Party (whose last government delivered consistent levels of economic growth and prosperity) cannot manage finances and just loves spending money. We can all bitch and moan about how unfair this is, but this is the reality that we face, true or not. So how I would pay for all of this is undoubtedly a challenge I would have to face and is the reason why it will never happen. It is just too expensive to stop women being abused by men. I know this is a fact – just one people are rarely willing to say. If we did say it, perhaps the country would express how appalling that sounds, perhaps they would react by demanding that we do pay for things like this. Perhaps if public services actually worked, people would be willing to pay higher taxes or be less terrified by the idea of government borrowing.* In

---

* People have been trained to be utterly terrified of government borrowing because it was rhetoric that suited Conservative governments. The truth is, of course, that all governments borrow money; they should seek to borrow to invest, like families do when they buy a house, rather than borrow to cover costs, like I do when I want new shoes. But borrowing in and of itself has been presented as a terrifying thing to do rather than a completely legitimate way for countries to operate their economy. Que sera, sera.

2016 the government undertook an analysis of the societal costs of domestic abuse and landed on the figure of £66 billion per year, made up of three elements:

- £47.3 billion: the estimated cost to those experiencing domestic abuse for the reduction in their quality of life due to the physical and emotional harms they experience
- £14.1 billion: the estimated cost to the economy of lost output
- £4.7 billion: the estimated cost of public and other services such as private civil and criminal legal representation and charitable services

Let's ignore the first massive figure because it is a technical definition of cost and is about the quality of life of victims, and frankly it should have done the same for perpetrators too because their quality of life is no doubt affected by their incidence of violence as well, but it's all a bit too amorphous and too conceptual for both politicians and the public to take on board. The second figure of £14.1 billion is a biggie – that is, lost economic output by victims of domestic abuse, too sick and insecure as a result of their experiences to be able to work at all or to their full potential. As a nation with such woeful productivity rates as the UK has today, you'd think someone might want to do something about a problem that was costing us £14.1 billion in lost output, they might think that investing in preventing this up front might be worth throwing a few quid at. If only. It is the final number that best makes the argument for spending. This is the actual cost we already incur (bear in mind this was 2016 – it will be much higher now) on dealing with the problem of domestic abuse. This isn't money we spend on preventing the problem; this is money we already, as taxpayers, are happy to spend on things like murder trials or children being put in care. This is money we spend on failure. We are happily shelling out nearly £5 billion on sewing up the gash in a woman's head after she was hit with the vacuum cleaner, while spending a much tinier amount on trying to stop her head being gashed in the first place. I don't really want my money going on putting kids in care when it could be used to get them and their mother housing and the welfare to maintain it thereafter. If the government invested even a fifth of this last pot of money, the smallest amount in the cost matrix, into prevention work we could probably halve the amount of money we were spending cleaning up after the crime and we would still be much better off.

We have no chance of achieving prevention and diversion without investing significantly more money into the processes and being bold about what they would look like. The question of how it will be paid for is another reason why politicians fail to act on things, because they think that the public will not wear the costs or for some reason they are too afraid of saying, 'Yes, we will borrow for the initial investments, or defund x, y and z to pay for it, because we will save money and even make money in the long run.' The problem is that the long run is too often not argued for enough when we are all fighting over the now.

The solutions in the perpetrator prevention arena can be debated, but the point I am seeking to make is that the honesty needed to try something new and different and possibly controversial is at present stymied by the fact that it is hard and will not show signs of progress quickly enough for election cycles for anyone to get a benefit. The fact that no politician can benefit electorally for this should not be the reason not to do it, slowly but surely, but I am telling you that it is. That, and the simple fact that we live in a patriarchy that doesn't care as much about women's pain as it does about men's. The cultural tentacles of men's control over women run so very deep in some cases that no matter what is tried, it fails. We tend to just ignore it and allow women to do the free labour of protecting themselves. Women offer very cheap solutions to governments in this and many other areas, like care. We just do the job of the police and the NHS for free ourselves.

After the murder of Sarah Everard there was a moment where women right across the country spoke about all the things they do each day to keep themselves safe. Women spoke of walking home with their keys laced through their fingers ready to use as a weapon if attacked. Girls talked about how they monitor their friends' movements on apps to make sure they get home after nights out. I have never in all my years of revelling at night not requested a friend text me as soon as she gets home, to tell me she is okay. When this was happening, I asked my husband if he had ever done similar with his mates. He looked at me dumbfounded. Of course he hadn't. He said he had no idea that women were doing all this micromanaging of their safety, and that if I had done this all my life, I must have spent hours and hours of time on it and that I could have spent that time and level of detail single-handedly making a feature-length stop-frame animation film or sewn the Bayeux Tapestry. Imagine the time I could have back if I thought that truly dangerous men were being monitored by someone else. Think of the national productivity uptick if women were not having to do this safety work – we could focus that time doing good.

The Tory government's response was to do an ad campaign and ask people not to be bystanders to the abuse of women. Imagine if the response to terrorism was an ad campaign about spotting terrorism. There is an entire government scheme called Prevent, which is about informing on and diverting people with extremist views that could lead to an act of terrorism. It has been controversial, and I am not here to discuss its merits, but the annual Home Office budget for Prevent is around £50 million. By comparison the Home Office committed (only starting in 2023) £18 million for programmes to divert domestic abuse perpetrators. If there are, as we know, around 1 million victims of domestic abuse each year, they can expect £18 each to fund prevention of the crimes against them. In 2023 there were 889,918 domestic abuse incidents reported to police (oddly excluding Devon and Cornwall) according to the ONS and we know this will only represent one in five cases because so many people do not report. In 2023 there were 6,817 cases referred to Prevent for extremist concerns. The crime that got funding of £50 million had less than 1 per cent of the cases of the crime that was allocated £18 million. Tell me again, oh dear government minister, how domestic abuse is a crime you take as seriously as terrorism.

In early 2024 James Cleverly, the then home secretary, said: 'Tackling violence against women and girls has been a priority for me for a long time. It is now a priority set out in the strategic policing requirement, meaning that VAWG is rightly considered to be as serious a focus as tackling terrorism.'

Obviously, I know this to be complete and utter bollocks, so minutes after he had made this statement in the House of Commons, I countered with the above statistics about the amount of money his own government department spends on the prevention of terrorism versus the prevention of violence against women and girls:

'The home secretary said that the strategic policing requirement is designed to make this issue as important as terrorism, but which police force in the country with a counter-terrorism unit has the same number of officers in that unit as it does specialists in violence against women and girls? Why did his department spend £50 million last year on 6,817 Prevent referrals to prevent people from ending up in terrorism, but £18 million on 889,918 police reports of domestic abuse? We have 6,000 on one side and nearly 1 million on the other; the Home Office spends £18 million on DV perpetrators and £50 million diverting terrorism perpetrators, and says, "We are taking it just as seriously."'

Now I will cut him some slack on his response; aside from being the actual home fucking secretary and the lead government official in charge of policy on domestic abuse, he will not have known these figures when I sprung them on him. He should but doesn't know anywhere near as much about the issue as I do, so I wasn't expecting a detailed response to my question based on facts and figures and reasons for the anomaly. I was hoping he might be honest with me and say that no government has ever taken this form of violence as seriously as others and it is going to take time and effort to get the two issues on a par. This would have been the honest, good politics answer of someone who had the intention to do the work. Do you, dear reader, think that is what I got back – honesty, pragmatism and just a touch of contrition? If only. What he actually said was: 'She makes a point about numbers of officers and budgets – I am not convinced that that is necessarily the most useful metric of the seriousness with which we take things.'

He is not convinced that resources expended on an issue are the metrics of how seriously we take things. I guess he's just hopeful that with no extra officers or budgets to prevent perpetrators, they will just stop on their own when we all live in a lovely, imagined world. One wonders why we spend so much on terrorism when we could save the taxpayer a pretty penny by just hoping that the tiny number of people who commit terrorist offences just recognise the error of their ways. The fact that he also tried to patronise me by implying that I didn't understand the way things work and was looking at the wrong data is quite something when both he and I know that if we were to compare my knowledge on the policing of both of these crimes with his, he would be in the Vauxhall Conference and I would be in the Premier League, just to put it in terms his manly brain can understand.

I honestly would prefer him to say the truth: 'Well, love, you know as well as I do that fighting terrorism, even though it kills way fewer people, harms fewer still, is a far better political platform to stand on, because it means we can scare the bejeezus out of people and look really tough. The public are more scared of terrorism than the beating or raping of women.'

I am not for one second saying that we shouldn't do all that we are doing to fight terrorism; I am simply asking that we also fight men's violence against women and girls with as much vigour. And if we won't do that, can we just be honest about why we won't rather than just repeatedly saying that we are? Politicians, stop spitting in our faces and telling us it's raining. The public are not idiots, and all this does is make people think that politics is morally bankrupt. Telling someone like me that we take terrorism and domestic abuse as seriously as each other is gaslighting, which, by the way, has become a much-overused phrase but, in this instance, stacks up. It tells a woman who has just been informed that the man who beat and raped her will not face any charges that she is imagining her poor treatment. If she had only thought to tell them that her husband was also being radicalised online by Isis jihadists and had been looking up the 'Jolly Roger' cookbook, he would now be in prison.

The fact that globally we don't care about domestic abuse as much as we care about terrorism has in many cases led to terrorist atrocities: men's violence against women not taken as seriously as it should and allowed to progress and advance to such extreme violence that they commit acts of terrorism. The man who attacked Westminster, killing five people on Westminster Bridge before he murdered the police officer Keith Palmer, had been so violent towards his wife that she had fled across the country from him. The terrorist who killed more than eighty people when he drove a truck into a crowd in Nice had a long history of abuse against women. One of the Boston Marathon bomber brothers had been arrested for domestic abuse. The man who killed three people in a Planned Parenthood clinic in Colorado had a long history of domestic abuse and of violence against women, and had previously been arrested for rape. The list could go on and on. Feminists have been trying to point out this connection for years and finally, in 2021, Project Starlight was set up to investigate the link. National Co-ordinator for Prevent, Detective Chief Superintendent Vicky Washington, said: 'Project Starlight has indicated a clear overrepresentation of domestic abuse experiences in the lives of those who are referred to us for safeguarding and support [for terrorism prevention].' The report also stated that, 'Whilst the data showed a similar prevalence of domestic abuse incidents for both men and women referred to Prevent, men were most often recorded as an offender and women as a victim of abuse. Children (those under 16) were most likely to be a witness.' The fact that we are not prioritising domestic abuse for both victims and perpetrators is literally causing terrorism. Since the findings of Starlight, I have seen absolutely no effort by ministers to improve responses to domestic abuse, or to change the way that we profile terrorism suspects.

* * *

Sorry if I have rambled on about quite how much we don't care about crimes of violence by men against women. What I am trying to highlight, if it was not clear, is just how bad politics can be when it pretends to care about an issue for the sake of how it looks rather than actually trying to change something.

I cannot express how well this could be done without properly hammering home this point: that allowing government departments and institutions like the police to simply say something matters when it clearly doesn't is everything we should fight against. If we hoped for more from our politics, we would expect that when presented with these platitudes about how much our representatives care about us it was done with a well-thought-through plan, with good data and measurable metrics and time-frames, which might show that the politicians were concerned more about the issue than about their own electability or the electability of their political party.

I have given just a few examples of things that could be done to actually improve this issue with regard to policing: have a measurable target, have a baseline of data that can be trusted, insist on priority and parity of resource, and ensure that every police force has a women's safety unit and a robust offender management service, as it would in a counter-terror unit. These are the policy responses that would work, and I could write a whole book about others that would work in other areas of policy like housing, welfare, children's safeguarding services, justice and the courts, teaching healthy relationships and safeguarding in schools to the next generation or health service responses to trauma. In every single area domestic abuse should be considered a priority but barely gets a mention. This book is not intended to be a policy pamphlet, so I won't explain to you what would work in each of these different sectors. What I am expressing is how the politics needs to be done with honesty and detail rather than bluster and ego.

If I didn't believe that better was possible and that politics was the only feasible vehicle for delivering change in women's safety, I can tell you now I would have stayed working in a women's refuge. The practice of policy in this area is so far away from the way it is spoken about with sorrow and care. We should hope for so much more from our politics than just expecting our politicians to say that they are sad for the families of murdered women. I don't want sorrow, I want action and graft. I want politics in this space, and frankly every other space, to deliver me better results and be honest with me and the public about what is not possible. I want to be able to tell people that, yes, something is going to cost money but that is okay because it will be worth it. Imagine during the pandemic if politicians had said, 'Sorry, we would pay for testing to get the economy moving again but it's too costly, so we've decided just to screw the economy.' I want to be able to say that because of money issues, we will have to take things slower than we would like, and to explain that coherently and expect good faith from those who lobby hard on these subjects.

I cannot end men's violence against women and girls. If I was given the job of dealing with this issue by a Labour government, I'd make mistakes and women would still die, children would still be taken into care and perpetrators would still get away with it, but I would make it better than it is, and I would try to explain along the way how I was doing it and what was expected. I would try to say when I got things wrong and missed targets I had dearly hoped to achieve. I wouldn't ever just say to someone challenging me on it that they were looking at the wrong metrics and they should look instead at these lovely shiny positive-looking metrics that I liked more. Look at me, I am such a good girl because fewer women died this year; ignore that thousands more nearly did, because I have this snake oil to sell you that does exactly what you hoped it would.

Governing isn't easy, changing things is really, really hard, but just pretending that you care more about it than you do and cherry-picking data that suits your agenda is the wrong way to do politics. The right way is to be transparent about what you are trying to achieve and honest about the processes, barriers and failings. I would never have won the trust of the public on the issue of violence against women and girls if I had simply made out that I was some world-beating superhero who was going to lie to them about the reality of the situation. Ultimately, I have to be willing to disappoint those with faith in me in order for them to truly trust me. Our politics is currently so far, far away from this as a practice that I worry if we can actually ever get it back to achieving such a level of honesty. If we don't, we will never put the attention into what needs doing differently and just try to find ways of saying something differently in order to con people.

I think it is possible to change this culture, and I dearly hope that in this area of policy I get the chance to prove it for what remains of my political career, both inside and outside of elected office. But you, the voter, have to do something, too; you have to allow the end result to be what you are striving for as well. You have to learn to obsess about the overall outcome not simply the individual outputs. You have to put aside some disappointments and, instead of hoping for a political scalp if something goes wrong, you have to push for an alternative solution to be presented. Chopping off the head of this minister or that secretary of state because something went wrong just makes the next bloke (it is usually a bloke) feel really terrified of trying to take a risk. Not a fear I would worry about, to be honest. I have found that if you truly believe in something and are willing to work hard at it, it doesn't really matter what your job title is. But most people in Westminster, Washington or the Bundestag do really worry about the letters before and after their names. We have to, as citizens, start rewarding effort to try as well as results achieved.

This may sound as if I think we should cut politicians too much slack because I don't like you moaning at me. Au contraire, I don't mind at all you moaning at me, but I hate that I am part of a system that rewards slavish loyalty and the ability to handle a tricky interview on behalf of your boss, rather than a dedicated public servant desperate to change something. We have, me included, grown too used to enjoying the political drama of a sacked minister or scandal that damages our political foes. I am sometimes giddy with excitement when the Tories are having a mare of a week. It's too easy to forget in such political intrigues that the only people who are truly hurt by crappy governance are those who need houses or are frightened for their kid's health and can't get the services they need.

We should focus our attention always on what is and isn't working and what we can all do to make that better. We must show our workings and trust the public to understand the detail of these efforts. We should tell people what is going wrong without always looking for an opportunity to score a political hit from that thing going wrong, and we should praise people not only when they achieve something but also when they tried to achieve something. We did this during the pandemic; I think we have the capacity and intelligence to now do it in a variety of circumstances.

In the policy area of men's violence against women I have grown so tired of systemic change being ignored because it is too hard and too long-term to bother about, with only minor changes and warm words being offered instead. There has been very little political incentive to do anything else and that has to change. This is not how our politics should be done; I have made it clear here, I hope, how we could do this differently, not just with policy but also how we approach talking about policy. If we actually want to tackle the challenges we face as a society we have all got to change the way we approach what we expect, how we interface with it, and understand that it will be hard but not impossible. Just declaring that it is too difficult and that we don't trust that it will ever change only gives politics an excuse to prove us right and deliver based on our expectations. I, for one, expect a shitload more.

8

What Is Working

I feel that in laying out what we need to do to make things better, I have not praised the good bits anywhere near enough. I learned long ago that if you want people to join you in making political change, then moaning incessantly and barking out tasks is the quickest way to stop them turning up for a second session of activism. I want and need you to believe in the possible even when politics has gone to hell in a handcart.

To put it simply, I have spent the first nine years of my elected life living under what went from bad ideology and false austerity to outright psychodrama and fascist-adjacent, couldn't-be-trusted-to-look-after-a-pot-plant lunacy. I was elected on to the local council in 2012 and to parliament in 2015. It hasn't been a pretty time, but if you were to ask if I thought it was so broken as to be unfixable the answer would be an emphatic 'hell, no'.

The reason I believe change is possible is because I have seen remarkable things happen in my time working in elected office, and every single bit of it comes from the ordinary citizen on the street. The vast majority of people aren't chasing popularity like politicians are, and they're a lot better for it. On the day I am writing this, it is a sunny Sunday in Birmingham. Yesterday, in one of my regular Saturday advice surgeries, where my constituents come and ask me for help with their problems, not one single person who walked through my door was there to seek something better for themselves. Everyone was there with a story to tell about their kids needing better, their neighbours they were worried about, or their sick and elderly parents being unable to access the care they needed. A woman with some very expertly done lip fillers bought me a bunch of lilies to say thank you for getting her pushed to the top of the housing list (even though this will still mean waiting around a year for a house). She had been the victim of some of the most violent domestic abuse I had ever heard of and I was scared that her life was still very much at imminent risk. She said the words, like so many before her have said, 'I'm not scared for me anymore, I can't feel any more pain, but my daughters, how would they cope if their mum was gone?' Another woman bought me a packet of doughnuts because she was worried I work too hard and don't get enough energy. She has suffered tyranny at the hands of her neighbours; all she could obsess about was the effect on her daughter's mental health. Another lovely young man, whose Irish heritage was written all over his dark-featured face, came to express concern about how his father who had cancer couldn't properly access the care he needed from his doctor. He had made complaints, got his dad on to what was allegedly a gold-standard framework and had arranged already for a specialist hospice nurse. There was nothing much else I could offer or do other than thank him and tell him he was a good son, dealing with what seemed like a stoic Irish father. I sympathised with him as I have one of those as well.

The final case felled me. I am a tough cookie, I've seen and heard terrible things, but the last person was a 34-year-old woman with terminal recurring cervical cancer. She came in with her mother; they needed rehousing. The woman's cancer had spread to her lungs and her rental property was damp and had black mould. She was also struggling with the stairs up to the flat where she lived with her three children. Her mother kept saying they could come to her, but she only had a one-bed flat and they needed to plan for an unknown future to ensure that the children were looked after if the worst happened. It transpired during the conversation that the mother of this woman had recently lost her son to drug addiction and her husband had also died within the year. At no point was this grandma asking for help and support for herself having faced such unimaginable loss and worry; all these women wanted was a chance to plan a future for these three little kids who might soon be motherless and homeless. They were utterly cheery throughout, never demanding, and in fact being self-deprecating about how they had messed up different forms and no wonder the council was being slow. When they left my office with my promise that I would try to help, I wept openly in front of John, my caseworker, and the lovely close-protection security guard who accompanies me. This woman was in a similar situation to my own family: my sister-in-law is living with terminal breast cancer and two kids under ten; when they needed to move out of their unsuitable social housing so that she could be cared for, my family were lucky enough to have been able to fund that. I wanted everything that these women wanted: I wanted to know that my little nephews would be okay in case of the worst thing happening; that they would be in a safe, secure home; that they were around their family; that we could get a place where my sister could eventually be housed only on the ground floor when the decline happened. I wept for the welfare state that wasn't there anymore, the housing that no longer exists to provide, even though my own family will never, ever be forced to rely on it. I wept because people are better and kinder than the politics they are up against.

Every single rape victim I have ever met utters the following phrase: 'I was one of the lucky ones because ...', usually followed by: 'I was raped by a stranger/I had a lovely police officer/my mum believed me when I told her about my dad/I had the evidence on my phone/I have a lovely caring husband/I have a good job.' Every rape victim believes, somewhat unbelievably, that they were lucky for some reason, because even in the face of their dreadful trauma they think about people who have it worse. They want to change the system for someone else. People are good and kind and want to use bad things that happen to help other people.

No one who came to see me in that perfectly normal morning surgery was thinking about how they could play the system for themselves; they were all there to try to improve the system for someone else that they loved, and in so doing for all the people who might need it. Yes, one in every hundredth person who comes to me for help is a ranting arsehole who merely hates the world, but they are the absolute tiny minority.

People have not been beaten by the system being broken, they have been activated. After my surgery I hotfooted it home, to quickly brush my hair and put on a pair of big earrings in a bid to look more dressy, and ran out of the door to go to the wedding vow renewal of a woman named Jhiselle. I met Jhiselle because her sister Bianca died falling from one of the tower blocks in Birmingham City centre. Bianca had been in a dangerously abusive relationship and Jhiselle campaigns for better investigations to happen in cases where women die suddenly when living with domestic abuse. We call them 'hidden homicides', when women die by suicide, substance misuse or in unexplained incidents having lived with years of abuse. At Jhiselle's wedding vow renewal I sat with Emma Ambler, whose twin sister and nieces were shot dead by the husband and father who should never have been granted a gun licence. With us tucking into curried goat from the buffet was Nour Norris, whose sister and niece were killed by her niece's violent partner; when they called 999 for help on the night of their murder, they were ignored. These women were all brought together for a celebration of love and hope for the future by their activism in the face of horror. Joining us was Anna Ryder, who, along with these women, started the Killed Women network. Anna turned up at my office to help leaflet in the 2017 election and basically never left; she is still listed in my phone as 'Keeno Anna' because she just kept rocking up to help. Working alongside me for years, she met all these brilliant women and started to organise them into a unified campaign group.

In the years of system shutdown, failure and the politics of division and hate, these women all danced together to '90s R&B hits, laughed and joked and delighted in each other's successes. Jhiselle is part of the movement that has changed the way we monitor sudden deaths in cases like her sister's. The system in our country is changing, slowly but surely, in her image. Emma has, along with others who have lost loved ones to gun violence, forced the government into a consultation on our nation's gun-licensing laws, and the Labour Party have agreed that, if in government, they will implement the changes she seeks. Nour fought for a coroner's hearing into the deaths of her sister and niece; she is now called on to train police forces and is on her way to seeing the introduction of Raneem's law (named after her niece), which will see specialist domestic abuse experts placed in every 999 call centre so the mistake that led to her family's loss will never happen again.

These women, who didn't know each other, were brought together by the politics of hope in the face of system failure and the most unimaginable grief and loss. They are, even in the worst of times, changing things.

These examples I have given you chart one single day in my political life. Every single day I meet people so amazing, so kind, so ordinary in their own eyes. The women led to activism by grief and loss do not spend their time obsessing about what folks are saying about them on Twitter. They roll their eyes at the ever-changing personnel at the Home Office; when one home secretary goes after another catastrophic political failure rather than through the ballot box, they just crack on getting to know the new one and keeping ties with the hardworking civil servants who are actually there to serve them not their stroppy ministers.

In fact, Anna Ryder and I, along with Zelda Perkins, one of the original Harvey Weinstein whistleblowers, once changed the law thanks to stupid culture war peacocking by the ministers in the Department for Education. Instead of worrying about the hundreds of thousands of kids who have gone missing from school since the Covid-19 pandemic lockdown, the DfE decided that the most pressing thing in need of legislation was the fact that there was a cancel culture springing up on our university campuses. They decided to pass a law that was purportedly about freedom of speech on campuses; in reality, it was just a chance to have another row about woke students. While the legislation was passing through the House of Commons, we saw an opportunity to talk about the silencing of victims of sexual abuse and harassment in our universities. We had for a number of years been in touch with students who had been abused by either staff or fellow students while at university and had been forced to sign harmful non-disclosure agreements (NDAs). In one case I cited in the Commons debate, a young woman was told where she could and couldn't walk around campus so she could avoid the student who had raped her; she was also told that if she made her case public, she would be kicked out of the university. Sick, right? We used the stupid culture war legislation to pass a law banning the use of NDAs in cases of sexual harassment at UK universities. It was very hard for the government to argue against our amendments to the law when they were making such a massive show about freedom of speech on campus.* I hate the piece of legislation that they were passing, it was a stupid waste of time in the culture wars they were desperate to stoke, but I skin the cat I have, and this was the only bill we had to work with. Keeno Anna, true to her name, drafted the amendment that eventually changed the law with ten minutes to go before the deadline on what felt like the back of a fag packet, after a rushed phone call with Zelda Perkins who had been campaigning on this very issue of university campus NDAs for the previous year. When we finally change the law to ban these agreements in the workplace too, I will call it Zelda's law – she has been fighting for this pretty much since she was silenced by the odious Weinstein, when she worked for him in the 1990s. But the law we changed on university campuses, this I want to name Anna's law. That bright-eyed, enthusiastic woman who turned up to a messy office in east Birmingham just

---

* They have, by the way, refused to pass this law for NDAs in the workplace.

to do a leaflet round went on to protect vulnerable people in every part of our country, and she did it by spinning political nonsense into political gold.

The reason Anna turned up to my office on that fateful day in 2017,* the reason I know any of the women I have cited as change-makers, is because we linked together through the press and social media. So much of the evidence gathering we do when we are trying to fight a campaign comes from the very thing we all bemoan as horrid and divisive. I could not have changed anything that I changed, raised any money for causes and campaigns, rallied so many people to our causes, without the help of brilliant campaigning and investigative journalists and the tool of social media. These are always at their finest when employed in the service of ordinary people rather than as the angry mouthpieces of those with too much power. Nothing is all bad, you see.

It is too easy to paint the press as all bad. I am often amazed at how liberal-thinking and self-identifying tolerant, educated people truly believe that other people are controlled by the press. Some people really think that 'the press', and by that they mean the tabloids and any newspaper or news media outlet that they don't agree with, is being controlled by some secret powerful cabal and in turn controls the masses. Of course, people are influenced by what they are told, everyone is; if you are getting your

---

* If truth be told, I think she came the first time because a lad she fancied was volunteering on that day; she came back the second day because she wanted to change things.

info from the *Guardian*, you just don't think you are being influenced. You are. It really pisses me off that smug people still think that the unwashed masses just believe and change their own beliefs and voting intention based on everything they read. Give people more bloody credit. People aren't made racist or sexist by newspapers unless they had a tendency for racism or sexism before. Newspapers tend to write what they think their readers already think. So in actual fact, the people decide what's in the newspaper, not the other way around.

However, in the recent post-Brexit era of batshit politics and outright mismanagement, the way I experience the press is as a schizophrenic force. It is either utterly brilliant and investigating all the right things, or it is acting as a sycophantic mouthpiece of its preferred political flavour. Here lies the difference between journalism and opinion. I like both, although if I could only have one it would be the former not the latter. Alas, one comes in much cheaper and seems to make much more money than the other.

If we want to talk about getting things right, there are hundreds of amazing pieces of journalism I could point to from the last decade that have truly changed the way the nation will vote without the political opinion of the journalist ever being revealed. I guess the starkest example of this is Amelia Gentleman's investigation into the Windrush scandal, which identified that the government was deporting or attempting to deport people to the Caribbean who had lived and worked in the UK for generations. Theresa May as home secretary wanted some low-hanging fruit – or, as I call them, people – to hit her targets on net migration. She basically needed to get rid of some folks because in her view too many were coming into the country. The Home Office identified that those who had come completely legally from the Caribbean could be that low-hanging fruit because of a quirk in the paperwork decades ago. Amelia Gentleman is married to Joe Johnson, brother of Boris Johnson; both at the time of the story were Conservative MPs so hardly first in line for calling for a people's revolution. Her journalism changed the course of history, because she listened to the voices of ordinary people and elevated their story.

Pippa Crerar, then at the *Daily Mirror*, and Paul Brand at ITV collectively uncovered the entire Partygate scandal, which hammered so many nails into Boris Johnson's coffin it was more nail than coffin. Many Boris fans will have accused them of being lefty liberals for uncovering the story. However, the final killer blow that buried Johnson in the end, and people often forget, was the work of a young rookie reporter called Noa Hoffman from famous liberal-mouthpiece newspaper the *Sun*, who uncovered the scandal of Boris Johnson essentially covering for Chris Pincher MP after his various indiscretions of the handsy variety.

The investigative journalism done into Baroness Michelle Mone and the various Covid-19 contracts by the brilliant journalist David Conn will have changed people's minds, not with ranting and opinion, but with cold, hard facts about how some people were made very rich out of a situation that made most people poorer. The stuff people write that does change minds is the reality, the facts; the opinions, it seems to me, just reinforce the views the audience already hold.

The trouble has been when opinions are dressed up as news, and GB News in the UK and Fox News in America, among others, are undoubtedly falling into this particular trap. While there are no doubt good journalists at both outlets, what they offer to their viewers is the comfort of their own views being reinforced or, in fact, an opportunity for anger and vitriol. Anger and vitriol are the outcome they seek. Fear makes money: it is easy to understand why greed and hatred manifest – it is much harder to fund kindness and reason. The press have a vital and important job to do in our democracy and without them none of the laws I have changed, or campaigns the citizens I work with have won, would have happened. Good press is to be treasured and opinions that are only there to create clicks for money should simply be ignored. Do not retweet them in anger!

If we can all survive through the horrific politics, the lies, spin and misdirection we have been put through both here in the UK and around the world of late, then things will be okay. If campaigning spirit can be found in the horror of a murder enabled by state failure, or good laws can be written accidentally because of moronic legislation, then surely there has to be nothing but hope. Imagine what is possible in times of *good* governance. Imagine how much these five women can achieve when they are not having to sidestep departments who don't prioritise them because they are too busy arguing with each other or fighting with imaginary foes. In just one day in my hometown, I saw enough hope, kindness and drive to change the world for ever. In just one day! Imagine what we could do in a decade if only we weren't so tired from all the problems, big and small, that stand in our way. Hell, yes, I have hope. I have hope because of people, not politicians. People really are smashing.

Conclusion

Let's be honest.

I fucking love politics. I have absolutely not one jot of time for people who lazily think that politics is all pointless or that it is only being done by the same boring bureaucrats who are so far away from the people who vote for them that it will never serve anyone but those who play the game. Seriously, if you have ever spouted anything like this then you, my friend, are both deeply unoriginal and also wrong. Politics is everything in your life. You think that you have agency over the choices you make – wrong again. People like me decided on what choices you could or couldn't make. People like me said who you could love, what kind of house you could live in. I decided on what kind of food would be available for you to eat, what you could study and where. I decided what you would be allowed to watch on telly while you cuddled up with the person who I said you could marry. It was up to me which kind of building you had that marriage ceremony in, and I said how late into the night you could buy a drink from the bar. I decided on all these things based on being one of you, knowing what I want for my family and how I wanted to live my life. I was unhappy with loads of the things that I saw playing out in my own personal and working life and I thought how lucky I was to live in a democracy that would make it possible for me to have a go at changing them.

What a gift that we so lazily dismiss as something that isn't about us. What a thing to live in a country where, if you don't like something, you can freely set about shifting it. Try living in Russia if you want an idea of how democracy can be used to tell you what to watch and who to love. If I was writing this book from Russia and had been even one tenth as critical of their elected leaders as I have been about ours, I would be currently evading the tip of an umbrella covered in Novichok. Rishi Sunak as PM was many things, but I don't think the fact that I have made clear that he is a dishonest, patronising fool who is shit at politics means that I will spend the rest of my days in a prison before having a mysterious heart attack. A low bar, I know. I'll give him something: he wasn't elected but he's not a psychotic despot.

I didn't set about writing a book on what is wrong with the state of our politics because I loathe it, but because I love it and want it to be nurtured and protected. We have all for far too long got high on the fumes of political drama and intrigue. We have all been co-opted into the idea that sharing our opinion online is somehow the same as doing the actual work it takes to change things. We have far too many times focused on *who* we don't like rather than *what* we don't like and what the hell we were going to do about it.

While we all took to our chosen platform to make clever quippy remarks about some politician we loathed, we encouraged them to behave the same. Contrary to popular belief, national politics reacts to the people way more than they know. Culture wars would never have been stoked and then exploited if politicians didn't think they would have traction. Recently, Rishi Sunak claimed that people protesting about the conflict in Gaza were creating mob rule. He said: 'There is a growing consensus that mob rule is replacing democratic rule. And we've got to collectively, all of us, change that urgently.' Yes, there are some idiots among those protesting on this issue. As many idiots as there were protesting (on both sides) during Brexit. Not just idiots: there are some people engaging in violent, racist and intimidatory behaviours while marching allegedly for peace. The vast majority of people who have pressed their political representatives on this issue are just upset about the deaths of many thousands of children in the war and don't like the idea of the UK government potentially backing genocide. The rotters. They are not a mob; they are simply people who are taking part in politics in a democracy. The ballot box is not their only outlet; they are free to protest and apply pressure on their MPs and councillors as they wish, within the laws.

The mob rule that I am worried about is the one that saw our government here in the UK, and those around the world, look to online forums spouting hate and conspiracy theories for inspiration in order to create political dividing lines and headlines rather than cracking on with their jobs. Jesus Christ, we had a politician in the UK who was dubbed the 'Cabinet Minister for Common Sense'! The role was taken up by Esther McVey and it would appear to me her job was to come out against imaginary policies that were not being proposed by anyone with any power. ESTHER MCVEY: SOCIALIST MADNESS OVER FOUR-DAY WEEK IS CATCHING ON, exclaimed the *Daily Express* newspaper, in an article where the minister for common sense took a pop at one local council in Cambridgeshire who have suggested they might one day in the future consider some staff working a four-day week. The common-sense approach to this would be to shrug and point out that loads of people already work a four-day week. My husband, when he was a white-van-driving, tabloid-reading, manual-working ordinary bloke on the street – the type I assume Ms McVey was attempting to appeal to with this tripe – shock horror . . . worked a four-day-week shift pattern. Those white van socialists must be stopped! The truth is, no bugger was suggesting we move to a four-day week, so it's a good job we had someone taking home a cushy ministerial salary to fight against it. Nonsense, more like.

A mob has very much been ruling: the Tory government. They spouted actual conspiracy theories about 15-minute cities, lied about how we are all going to be taxed to eat meat, and refused to call out racism within their ranks for what it is, in case they pissed off the people on Twitter with dog avatar faces.

What I find absolutely shocking about the fact that the culture wars were allowed to take such hold in cabinet is that so much of the online dissent about various culture war issues is so clearly and evidently being manufactured by the bot accounts of bad-faith and bad state actors. The government must have known that, what with them being in charge of the nation's security and all, and yet seemingly, while claiming that they were opposed to Russia and Iran, they in my view lapped up every delicious morsel of Kool-Aid sent by authoritarian propagandists. I guess when you can't be bothered to do your job, mobs and despots provide a little pleasant distraction. I am far less frightened of people who are protesting against Benjamin Netanyahu than I was of the transport minister spouting conspiracy theories from his conference pulpit.

It doesn't have to be this way. A little bit of critical thinking and, frankly, gentle ribbing about the idiocy are our best defence against this bullshit. The reaction loop and Outrage Olympics have got to stop. When Birmingham was described by an idiot from Fox News as a place taken over by Muslims that was a no-go area for white people, the response of the people in my city was not outrage and anger, it was funny photos of them outside Mecca bingo halls and pictures of jars wrapped in gingham cloth with gags about how even our jam had to wear a hijab. I salute the people of Birmingham! The government only played this game because we played along. They want us baying for blood. Pack it in.

Politics should be and can be again about what is

delivered for the people, but the people – that's you – should not simply expect to have stuff offered to them without effort on their part. It's on all of us to end the rot of allowing ministers to simply make proclamations, talk in pointless platitudes and then deliver nothing. Yes, we can do this at the ballot box by getting rid of the worst-offending charlatans, but we also have to sign up to a new way of thinking about what politics is for and who does it.

Politics is not something just done by politicians; each and every one of us genuinely has the power to change the way things are. If you don't like something, make an effort to change it. Be like Erin Brockovich, Alan Bates, Doreen Lawrence and the Hillsborough families. Failing starting a nationwide campaign that is so dramatic they will literally make a film about it, the easiest way we can make our politics better is to change our expectations. Don't assume that politics and political decisions are easy, or that wholesale reform can happen overnight, but do expect to be given a detailed plan and timeframe and then make sure you keep up the pressure about whatever it is you want to see changed.

Write to your representatives and ask what exactly they are going to do about an issue, not just what they think. In many cases they will be able to do absolutely nothing other than represent your views in parliamentary debates and push the people who have the power to do more. One of the worst things I felt about resigning from the Labour frontbench to vote for a ceasefire in Gaza was that I was heralded as a hero for doing something that took me literally less than one minute. Sure, there was a whole lot of agonising and work that led up to that moment, and a lot of corresponding and listening to thousands of people, but ultimately voting or proclaiming something is the very least I could do. Up your expectations!

Don't just fall for a rabble-rousing clip put out by a parliamentarian, ask: 'What's next?' I was so frustrated by how little effort it took me to vote for a ceasefire that I felt I had to do more. I set about raising tens of thousands of pounds to fund aid for the region; I worked with doctors from Gaza and the West Bank to ensure that they could be brought to parliament to speak about what was happening on the ground. I basically became the go-to politician for advice on getting people out of Gaza through the Rafah crossing, as so many of the initial cases who escaped were my constituents. I set about helping with cases from elsewhere in the country. Still today as you read this, someone in Palestine, or in Warrington, is emailing me and sending details of a family member of a British Gazan they want to get out. None of it will ever be enough, but the desire to do something, matched by the guilty sense of being heralded for such little effort, led me to action. Be wary of politicians who want you to polish their halos because they deigned to have an opinion on something and put out a clip on the socials. It's fine for them to do that ... just a bit of follow-up on the plan wouldn't go amiss. I see a lot of pontificating on the issue of Gaza and very little actual work.

It is not an easy sell, but we should praise work well done and find a way as a society to be more forgiving of the complexities of making change and political progress happen. I am not asking you to send love bombs to MPs, but the truth is that it is a hard job where you get a shedload of criticism even if you try your best. I get way more fan mail than hate mail (bear in mind I am one of the most abused MPs in the country) and honestly it keeps me going; it makes me want to work harder and impress people more. That said, I am not asking for MPs to get loads of fan mail, I am simply asking that we be allowed to make the case for things, be able to make mistakes and then be given the space to apologise for them. I don't mean when we have been caught with our pants down or our hands in the till – knock yourselves out shouting at an MP for that. I mean in big public policy changes. I am so sick of the spin and the questions going unanswered because telling the truth about why some things are the way they are is so unpalatable. We have allowed a situation to arise where mistakes and lies are all considered the same, and so it's just become easier to at best obfuscate and at worst barefaced mislead.

Some policies work, some don't. Some are cruel and dangerous; most are just an effort to try our best in a bad or crisis situation. There needs to be a difference in how these are seen. Some are a U-turn based on dreadful decisions initially made, some are a reasonable course correction. Screaming that politicians are U-turning or are completely useless when they change course just encourages bad behaviour, not good. Why bother to try when the end result is always vitriol or bad headlines? Liz Truss's mini-budget deserved wild howls of contempt; Conservatives raising

National Insurance fees to fund social care (which it didn't) after promising not to raise taxes didn't, because something needed to give at the time. I understand that there are manifestos for elections and politicians should try to stick to them, but the absolute truth is that sometimes the facts and figures are not equal to the hopes. Just like in your own life perhaps, when you changed course after falling accidentally pregnant, or were made redundant, or there was a global financial crisis. Shit happens.

I think that the public want politicians to answer the questions they are asked; I think they want to be told about things going well or not so well. Yes, we all like a bit of scandal or a political coup to keep things spicy, but that stuff will always exist because politicians are people and people are fallible, and if you are fallible and happen to work in a building with a hundred journalists in it then expect that to be writ large. When it comes to the job of actually governing, funding services and making social change, my God do we need a better way of talking about it. When a minister launches a new programme of renewal in the north, for example, instead of making out like the streets of Sunderland will now be paved with gold, and it will be just like that imagined time where things were better (even though they weren't) and you'll probably get a more beautiful spouse because of it and your kid will get a first from Oxford, perhaps we could just say, 'This is the first step in what we hope will be many more, but we are starting with skills gaps and making sure that there is a place for kids in Sunderland either to study their A-levels or to get a decent apprenticeship. It won't be perfect and it's going to take a long time for the policy to bear fruit that we hope will grow, but I promise we are going to try.' There is no sentence I say to my constituents more than: 'I don't know if I can help with this, I think the likeliest answer I will get is no, but I tell you what, I promise I will try.' No one has ever, in a decade of my saying it, replied to me, 'Do or do not, there is no try' because my constituents are more realistic than Jedi extremist Yoda. They understand because they are not thick!

Politicians can be disappointing; they can make it seem as if politics is a game about their careers and fortunes rather than just a job that has to be done well. The worst case I have ever seen of this was maddeningly about the issue of child sexual abuse. I was hosting an event in parliament a year after the publication of the Independent Inquiry into Child Sexual Abuse. This was a seven-year-long inquiry that took evidence from thousands and thousands of people who had been sexually abused in childhood and ignored by institutions such as the Church or children's homes. The inquiry made a series of detailed recommendations, all of which were not realised or even committed to by the government a year on from the end of the process. The Home Office dragged their feet in some cases because the recommendations would take time to implement. Fair enough, they should have just said this. There were other recommendations they didn't want to do but they weren't brave enough to admit that either. Overall, though, the reason the government had nothing to offer is because this simply wasn't a priority for the department that was sweating all of its assets and political capital on stopping small-boat crossings.

The event was essentially to push for action on the recommendations. I was hosting and we had invited the then home secretary, James Cleverly, to speak. Theresa May, who had been the home secretary at the time the inquiry began and who was ultimately responsible for getting it off the ground, was also due to speak. To be fair to her, she deserves some praise for her efforts in the role. On hearing that I was going to introduce the home secretary, his office began to panic about what I might say, as if I am some sort of savage who doesn't know how to behave. They started to ask if someone else could do it, perhaps someone from his office. They obviously didn't say this to me, but instead to the victims' group who were organising the event. They basically threatened not to come, because they didn't want me and Theresa May giving James Cleverly side-eye about how little he had achieved. Imagine in the face of child abuse victims who have spent seven years baring their souls in the hope of a new dawn for children who are being abused still, you care more about how you will look as the home secretary than you do about making the changes needed. Now, maybe James Cleverly knew nothing of these goings-on and it was just worried officials trying to dodge embarrassment for their boss, but when the outcome you are fretting about is the headline for the politician not the fucking child abuse perpetrated then everything about our politics has gone south.

Politicians want to look good because they want to get

elected, but looking good has replaced being good, which is actually what will ultimately get you re-elected, and if it doesn't manage that because your party is so toxic regardless of how brilliant you are, then at least you will have achieved an actual task. I pray for a time when politicians are willing to look bad and face decent, honest, good-faith scrutiny like grown-ups. My predecessor in the seat of Birmingham Yardley, Estelle Morris, was the Labour Secretary of State for Education. She resigned from the position because she didn't feel she was doing a good enough job. I actually think she was wrong and was probably the last really decent education secretary we had as a country, but can you imagine such a thing? By today's standards, Estelle Morris would just bluster her way through and pick a statistic that she liked, or worse still demand praise for a job badly done.

Perhaps, as Gillian Keegan, the Secretary of State for Education in the Sunak government, would say: 'Does anyone ever say: "You know what, you've done a fucking good job, because everyone else has sat on their arse and done nothing?" No signs of that, no?'

A little bit of both approaches might not go amiss. Estelle genuinely judged herself against outcomes achieved and showed immense dignity in thinking children in the country deserved better, and Gillian did have a point that you get no praise even when you try to do your best, so what's the point in trying? I might suggest to Ms Keegan, though, that anticipating praise for finally acting on a failure was expecting people to be grateful for the basics, while their

kids were out of school because the buildings were crumbling dangerously in the wake of years of disinvestment in
our education infrastructure.

If we truly want to see deeds not words for the problems
we face, I think there needs to be considerably more space
allowed for discussion and debate about what those deeds
might be and how we are all going to do our part to make
them happen. Expecting just the 650 people elected to
deliver everything is the way to absolute disappointment.
Like in the pandemic, we all rolled up our sleeves. There
will always be lazy bastards who don't do their bit and,
instead of making them the sole focus of our ire at the
unfairness of it, we should enjoy being virtuous. As my
late mom used to say, 'Would you swap places with them?
Being you is its own reward.' Few things annoy me more
than people who come and make demands on me who
are not willing to try to do something themselves. This is
a minority, to be fair; most people come and see an MP
when they have sweated every bloody asset they have and
are left helpless. But when people come and ask me to intervene because their neighbour is noisy, the first question I
ask is: have you asked them to pack it in? Often the answer
is no. I will help almost anyone, with almost anything, but
I will not do something for you that you can do yourself.
You might need some support and I will provide it, but I
do expect some effort on your part.

To get politicians actually to commit to more than the
most basic actions, you are going to have to put in some
effort. There's no need to be demanding but you might

need to be politely persistent. Nothing makes me want to get cracking on a task or a policy like someone who has come to me with a possible solution rather than just a grievance. Someone who is enthusiastically trying to get things done is bloody infectious. I'll walk the streets with them in the pissing rain on a Friday night getting their campaign message out. Angry, non-specific cries of 'more must be done, and you'd better do it' wouldn't get me walking the streets on a sunny afternoon.

Focusing on the outcome that you seek from your politicians will make the politics of our country focus on outcomes for us all. Politics absolutely does deliver good things for people; it has changed my life in immeasurable ways. Good politics has provided me with a safety net (albeit pretty holey at the moment) that means I will likely never starve; it saved my life and didn't send me an unpayable bill for the effort. Politics kept me safe when I was a victim of crime; it built me a road to get me to my loved ones (although I now have to wait in a longer queue to see the ones who live in France). Good politics literally gave me freedom as a woman to dare not just to vote, but to be voted for. Like I said, I love it. But we need the truth to come back into politics if we're going to get anywhere.

Acknowledgements

I dedicated this book to Holly Lynch, the MP for Halifax. You may not have heard of her and that is partially what is wrong with politics because in my view she is the best the building has to offer. Kind, clever, loyal and funny. I wouldn't have got through the last few years of political madness without her and some notable others who I won't list because I'll forget someone and that will be chalked up. Chris Elmore can have a mention as he keeps the little band of my Westminster best friends in check with his morning voting instructions.

This is the fourth book I have written in the last decade and I simply cannot believe it. It's all thanks to Laura Macdougall from United Agents who set me on this authorial path. I would still never be so bold as to refer to myself as an author; maybe one day. Also, a shout-out to Olivia Davies at United whose efficiency knows no bounds.

Holly Harris, my editor, is, in my view, the best in the business; she is both light-touch and not backwards in coming forwards when she wants a new direction. This book was born entirely from her vision. Thanks to all those who end up working on my books – there are way more people than you'd think! In Editorial, particular thanks to Sam Stocker, Lorraine Jerram and Charlotte Atyeo.

Thanks to Emma Harrow, Sabah Khan, Hannah Paget and all the marketing and PR team at Simon & Schuster. You tolerate my ignorance of the world of publishing and the annoying rules about elections and balance that have to be managed in my case.

To all the book festivals and independent bookshops that make the publishing bit of my life so fun. A special shout-out to Nicola Tuxworth of Cheltenham Festivals, who has become a firm friend and looked after me following the trauma detailed in this book, and to Jo James who is simply wonderful. To the Heath Bookshop in Kings Heath, Birmingham – thanks for giving us a local bookshop and also for looking after my kid after school in your lovely spot.

Thanks to my staff who, I hope you can see from this book's account of the UK/US withdrawal from Afghanistan, are some of the best people in the world. They go above and beyond to serve the people of Birmingham Yardley and deserve much better than to be described by lots of news reporting as 'spiralling MPs' expenses'. They are people who work very hard with little reward or recognition. To Katherine, John, David, Olivia, Apollo, Caroline, Anna and Jane, and all the volunteers, thank you so very much.

I must thank my tight-knit group of girlfriends, none of whom will read the book or any book I write, who roll their eyes when asked questions about me by others. The fact that they keep me separate is a gift.

To Tom, my husband and co-pilot in what can only be described as the best, safest and healthiest relationship I've ever come across. I'd one day like to write a book about how to have a happy marriage but he wouldn't allow the intrusion. (Top tip: only live together for half the week.) To Harry and Danny, who know fine well that if I wrote a book about good parenting, I'd have to lie through my teeth. Thanks for tolerating my adequate parenting. As a feminist who lives only with boys, I'm glad it's these ones.

Thanks finally to my dad, who cares so deeply about politics that I have no choice but to try to protect it.

Index